LEVEL THIRTEEN

DECIMALS, FRACTIONS, AND THE METRIC SYSTEM

Developmental Mathematics

Solution Manual

CONCEPTS & BASIC SKILLS

13

L. George Saad, Ph. D.
Professor Emeritus
Long Island University

Date _____

1 FRACTIONAL UNITS

- Fold a sheet of paper into two equal parts.
  Each part is one-half of the whole.

- Fold a sheet of paper into three equal parts.
  Each part is one-third of the whole.

- Fold a sheet of paper into four equal parts.
  Each part is one-fourth of the whole.

APPLICATIONS

a.

The whole consists of 5 equal parts.
Each part is __one-fifth__ of the whole.

b.

The whole consists of 6 equal parts.
Each part is __one-sixth__ of the whole.

c.

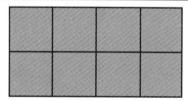

The whole consists of 8 equal parts.
Each part is __one-eighth__ of the whole.

d.

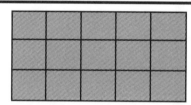

The whole consists of 15 equal parts.
Each part is __one-fifteenth__ of the whole.

e.

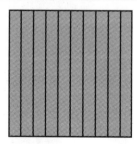

The whole consists of 10 equal parts,
Each part is __one-tenth__ of the whole.

f.

The whole consists of 100 equal parts,
Each part is __one-hundredth__ of the whole.

2

Example 1.

The whole is divided into 5 equal parts.
3 parts are colored.

Each part is one-fifth of the whole.
We say 3 fifths are colored.

We mean that 3 fifths of the whole figure are colored.

Example 2.

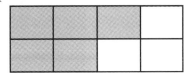

The whole is divided into 8 equal parts.
5 parts are colored.

Each part is one-eighth of the whole.
We say 5 eighths are colored.

We mean that 5 eighths of the whole figure are colored.

APPLICATIONS

Each figure is divided into equal parts.
What fraction of the figure is shaded?

a.
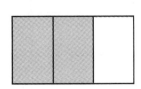
2 thirds

b.
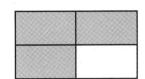
3 fourths

c.

2 fifths

d.
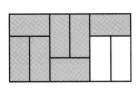
7 ninths

e.
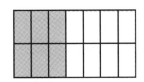
6 fourteenths

f.
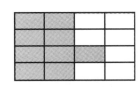
9 sixteenths

g.
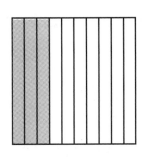
3 tenths

h.
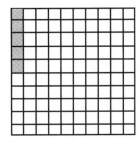
5 hundredths

i.
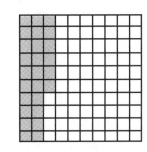
26 hundredths

© Copyright by L. George Saad

2 WRITING FRACTIONS

Example 1.

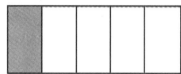

The figure is divided into 5 equal parts.
One part is colored.
- We say "One-fifth of the figure is colored."
- For 1 fifth we write $\frac{1}{5}$.

Example 2.

The figure is divided into 3 equal parts.
One part is colored.
- We say "One-third of the figure is colored."
- For 1 third we write $\frac{1}{3}$.

APPLICATIONS

Each figure is divided into equal parts.
What fraction of the figure is shaded?

a.

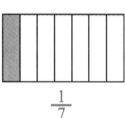

$\frac{1}{7}$

b.

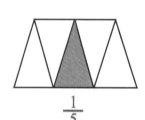

$\frac{1}{5}$

c.

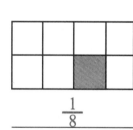

$\frac{1}{8}$

d.

$\frac{1}{6}$

e.

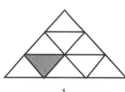

$\frac{1}{9}$

f.

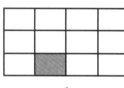

$\frac{1}{12}$

g.

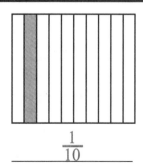

$\frac{1}{10}$

h.

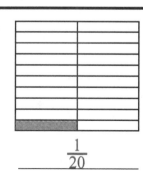

$\frac{1}{20}$

i.

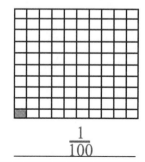

$\frac{1}{100}$

Example 3.

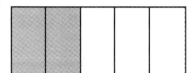

The figure is divided into 5 equal parts. Two parts are colored.

- We say "Two-fifths of the figure is colored."
- For 2 fifths we write $\frac{2}{5}$.

Example 4.

The figure is divided into 6 equal parts. Three parts are colored.

- We say "Three-sixths of the figure is colored."
- For 3 sixths we write $\frac{3}{6}$.

APPLICATIONS

Each figure is divided into equal parts.
What fraction of the figure is colored? What fraction of the figure is blank?

a.

Colored: $\frac{2}{3}$

Blank: $\frac{1}{3}$

b.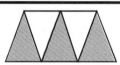

Colored: $\frac{3}{5}$

Blank: $\frac{2}{5}$

c.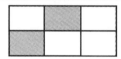

Colored: $\frac{2}{6}$

Blank: $\frac{4}{6}$

d.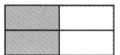

Colored: $\frac{2}{4}$

Blank: $\frac{2}{4}$

e.

Colored: $\frac{3}{9}$

Blank: $\frac{6}{9}$

f.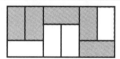

Colored: $\frac{5}{9}$

Blank: $\frac{4}{9}$

g.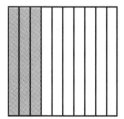

Colored: $\frac{3}{10}$

Blank: $\frac{7}{10}$

h.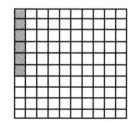

Colored: $\frac{6}{100}$

Blank: $\frac{94}{100}$

i.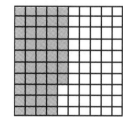

Colored: $\frac{47}{100}$

Blank: $\frac{53}{100}$

Date _____

3 WHOLES AND FRACTIONS

Example 1.
   You have 1 gallon and $\frac{1}{2}$ gallon of gas in the tank of your car.

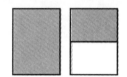

Discussion:
   You say "I have one and one-half gallons of gas."
   You write $1\frac{1}{2}$ to represent 1 and $\frac{1}{2}$ or $1 + \frac{1}{2}$.

   Similarly you write: $3\frac{2}{5}$ to represent 3 and $\frac{2}{5}$ or $3 + \frac{2}{5}$

   $5\frac{3}{7}$ to represent 5 and $\frac{3}{7}$ or $5 + \frac{3}{7}$

   $9\frac{7}{10}$ to represent 9 and $\frac{7}{10}$ or $9 + \frac{7}{10}$

   $38\frac{19}{100}$ to represent 38 and $\frac{19}{100}$ or $38 + \frac{19}{100}$

APPLICATIONS

1. The figures in each box are the same size. One of the figures is divided into equal parts. Write the number represented by the shaded area.

    $2\frac{1}{4}$

    $3\frac{3}{8}$

2. Write the number:
   a. 1 and 1 third $1\frac{1}{3}$ b. 3 and 1 fifth $3\frac{1}{5}$

   c. 5 and 1 seventh $5\frac{1}{7}$ d. 10 and 1 tenth $10\frac{1}{10}$

   e. 8 and 1 tenth $8\frac{1}{10}$ f. 73 and 1 hundredth $73\frac{1}{100}$

   g. 7 and 2 thirds $7\frac{2}{3}$ h. 9 and 5 sevenths $9\frac{5}{7}$

   i. 9 and 5 tenths $9\frac{5}{10}$ j. 2 and 7 hundredths $2\frac{7}{100}$

   k. $7 + \frac{1}{2}$ $7\frac{1}{2}$ l. $3 + \frac{2}{7}$ $3\frac{2}{7}$

   m. $4 + \frac{3}{10}$ $4\frac{3}{10}$ n. $9 + \frac{17}{100}$ $9\frac{17}{100}$

Example 2.

The figures to the right are the same size.
One figure and $\frac{1}{3}$ of the other are colored.

The one whole may be considered as 3 thirds.
4 thirds are colored.

$$1\frac{1}{3} = \frac{3}{3} + \frac{1}{3} = \frac{4}{3}$$

Example 3.	Example 4.
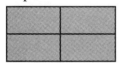	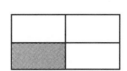
$1\frac{1}{4} = \frac{4}{4} + \frac{1}{4} = \frac{5}{4}$	$2\frac{2}{3} = \frac{6}{3} + \frac{2}{3} = \frac{8}{3}$

APPLICATIONS

1. Write the missing number:

a.

$$1\frac{2}{5} = \frac{7}{5}$$

b.

$$4\frac{2}{3} = \frac{14}{3}$$

c.

$$2\frac{1}{6} = \frac{13}{6}$$

d.

$$3\frac{1}{4} = \frac{13}{4}$$

2. Write the answer:
   a. How many halves are in $7\frac{1}{2}$?   15
   b. How many fifths are in $8\frac{3}{5}$?   43
   c. How many sixths are in $7\frac{5}{6}$?   47
   d. How many tenths are in $6\frac{9}{10}$?   69
   e. How many hundredths are in $7\frac{6}{100}$?   706
   f. How many hundredths are in $3\frac{19}{100}$?   319

3. Write the missing number:
   a. $2\frac{2}{3} = \frac{8}{3}$ b. $3\frac{2}{5} = \frac{17}{5}$ c. $5\frac{3}{4} = \frac{23}{4}$

   d. $5\frac{4}{7} = \frac{39}{7}$ e. $9\frac{3}{7} = \frac{66}{7}$ f. $7\frac{5}{8} = \frac{61}{8}$

   g. $4\frac{9}{10} = \frac{49}{10}$ h. $20\frac{7}{10} = \frac{207}{10}$ i. $3\frac{7}{100} = \frac{307}{100}$

4   TENTHS

- If you divide a figure into 10 equal parts, each part is 1 tenth of the whole figure, and 10 tenths = 1 whole.

- 1 tenth may be written as $\frac{1}{10}$, 7 tenths as $\frac{7}{10}$.

- 13 tenths may be written $\frac{13}{10}$ or $1\frac{3}{10}$.
  29 tenths may be written $\frac{29}{10}$ or $2\frac{9}{10}$.

- A 3-place numeral represents a number that consists of hundreds, tens, and ones. As an example:

  $$325 = 3 \text{ hundreds} + 2 \text{ tens} + 5 \text{ ones}$$

Tens	Ones	Tenths
3	2	5

- You can go on to create a new place for tenths. The numeral written in the boxes to the right represents: 6 tens + 4 ones + $\frac{7}{10}$ or $64\frac{7}{10}$.

Tens	Ones	Tenths
6	4	7

- The numeral written in the boxes to the right represents: 8 tens + 0 ones + $\frac{5}{10}$ or $80\frac{5}{10}$.

Tens	Ones	Tenths
8	0	5

- The numeral $39\frac{7}{10}$ is written as shown in the boxes to the right.

Tens	Ones	Tenths
3	9	7

- The numeral $40\frac{8}{10}$ is written as shown in the boxes to the right.

Tens	Ones	Tenths
4	0	8

In such cases we usually use a period to seperate fractions from wholes. This period is called a "decimal point".

a.
Tens	Ones	Tenths
3	8	4
is written 38.4 and
Tens	Ones	Tenths
5	0	6
is written 50.6.

b. $38\frac{4}{10}$ may be written 38.4 and is read 38 and 4 tenths.

c. 0.3 is read 3 tenths   d. 0.3 is the same as $\frac{3}{10}$

e. 0.8 is read 8 tenths   f. 0.8 is the same as $\frac{8}{10}$

g. 1.2 is read 1 and 2 tenths   h. 1.2 is the same as $1\frac{2}{10}$ or $\frac{12}{10}$

APPLICATIONS

1. Use a decimal point to write the numeral presented in the boxes.

a.
Ones	Tenths
	8
= __0.8__

b.
Ones	Tenths
4	9
= __4.9__

c.
Ones	Tenths
1	7
= __1.7__

d.
Ones	Tenths
6	
= __6.0__

e.
Tens	Ones	Tenths
5	3	2
= __53.2__

f.
Tens	Ones	Tenths
9	2	6
= __92.6__

g.
Tens	Ones	Tenths
6	0	7
= __60.7__

h.
Tens	Ones	Tenths
4		8
= __40.8__

2. Use a decimal point to write the following numerals:

a. $\frac{8}{10}$ = 0.8

b. $\frac{7}{10}$ = 0.7

c. $\frac{1}{10}$ = 0.1

d. $\frac{4}{10}$ = 0.4

e. $\frac{9}{10}$ = 0.9

f. $\frac{6}{10}$ = 0.6

g. $2\frac{3}{10}$ = 2.3

h. $6\frac{7}{10}$ = 6.7

i. $8\frac{5}{10}$ = 8.5

j. $3\frac{1}{10}$ = 3.1

k. $3\frac{2}{10}$ = 3.2

l. $19\frac{8}{10}$ = 19.8

m. $\frac{39}{10}$ = 3.9

n. $\frac{87}{10}$ = 8.7

o. $\frac{138}{10}$ = $13\frac{8}{10}$ = 13.8

p. $\frac{107}{10}$ = $10\frac{7}{10}$ = 10.7

q. $\frac{311}{10}$ = $31\frac{1}{10}$ = 31.1

r. $\frac{706}{10}$ = $70\frac{6}{10}$ = 70.6

3. Write how you read the following numerals:

a. 0.3 is read __three-tenths.__

b. 0.9 is read __nine-tenths.__

c. 2.5 is read __two and five-tenths.__

d. 8.8 is read __eight and eight-tenths.__

e. 17.6 is read __seventeen and six-tenths.__

f. 30.2 is read __thirty and two-tenths.__

g. 100.1 is read __one hundred and one-tenth.__

h. 298.4 is read __two hundred ninety-eight and four-tenths.__

Level 13

GROUPING AND EXCHANGING

How do you write the numeral which represents 39 tenths?
You may use boxes as shown to the right.

Ones	Tenths
	39

But 39 tenths must be grouped into 3 ones and 9 tenths,
and is written as shown to the right.

Ones	Tenths
3	9
= 3.9

Similarly:

a.

Ones	Tenths
5	14
=
Ones	Tenths
6	4
= 6.4

b.

Ones	Tenths
8	67
=
Ones	Tenths
14	7
=
Tens	Ones	Tenths
1	4	7
= 14.7

c.

Ones	Tenths
7	50
=
Ones	Tenths
12	0
=
Tens	Ones	Tenths
1	2	0
= 12.0

Example 1.

Write 89 tenths in the standard form.

Discussion:

The standard form is hundreds, tens, ones, and tenths.

89 tenths must be grouped into 8 ones and 9 tenths, and is written 8.9.

Similarly:

a. 73 tenths = __7.3__   b. 51 tenths = __5.1__   c. 289 tenths = __28.9__

Example 2.

How many tenths are in 8?

Discussion:

You know that there are 10 tenths in 1. Thus, 8 = 80 tenths.

Similarly:

a. 5 = __50 tenths__   b. 3 = __30 tenths__   c. 29 = __290 tenths__

Example 3.

How many tenths are in 5.3?

Discussion:

5 = __50 tenths__   5 and 3 tenths = __53 tenths__

Similarly:

a. 3.7 = __37 tenths__   b. 8.9 = __89 tenths__   c. 12.5 = __125 tenths__

APPLICATIONS

1. Study each example, and rewrite the number in the lower boxes:

a.

Ones	Tenths
	35

is written

3	5

b.

Ones	Tenths
7	16

is written

8	6

c.

Ones	Tenths
3	26

is written

5	6

d.

Tens	Ones	Tenths
	1	83

is written

	9	3

e.

Tens	Ones	Tenths
	9	27

is written

1	1	7

f.

Tens	Ones	Tenths
5	7	38

is written

6	0	8

2. Write in the standard form:

   a. 8 tenths   =   0.8
   b. 9 tenths   =   0.9
   c. 38 tenths =   3.8
   d. 27 tenths =   2.7
   e. 50 tenths =   5.0
   f. 80 tenths =   8.0
   g. 127 tenths =   12.7
   h. 108 tenths =   10.8
   i. 130 tenths =   13.0
   j. 190 tenths =   19.0

3. Change into tenths:

   a. 5   =   50   tenths
   b. 7   =   70   tenths
   c. 4.2 =   42   tenths
   d. 3.1 =   31   tenths
   e. 14   =   140 tenths
   f. 29   =   290 tenths
   g. 14.8 =   148 tenths
   h. 30.4 =   304 tenths

4. Compare the two numbers:

   a. Which is larger, 13 or 129 tenths?

      129 tenths = 12.9   13 is larger than 12.9   So, 13 is larger than 129 tenths

   b. Which is smaller, 42 or 425 tenths?

      425 tenths = 42.5   42 is smaller than 42.5.   So, 42 is smaller than 425 tenths

5. Arrange the given numbers:

   a. Rewrite the following numbers in descending order:

      368 tenths, $36\frac{9}{10}$, and 36   36.9, 36.8, 36

   b. Rewrite the following numbers in ascending order:

      2.4, $\frac{21}{10}$, and 23 tenths   2.1, 2.3, 2.4

Level 13

5   ADDING

You know that:

   2 tenths + 3 tenths = 5 tenths

Similarly

   a.   3 tenths + 5 tenths =   __8__ tenths

   b.   8 tenths + 1 tenth =   __9__ tenths

   c.   4 tenths + 2 tenths =   __6__ tenths

   d.   2 tenths + 3 tenths=   __5__ tenths

You know that:

   4 tenths + 8 tenths = 12 tenths

   12 tenths must be grouped into 1 and 2 tenths.

Similarly:

   a.   7 tenths + 8 tenths = 15 tenths = 1 and 5 tenths

   b.   8 tenths + 4 tenths = __12__ tenths = __1 and 2 tenths__

   c.   6 tenths + 7 tenths = __13 tenths = 1 and 3 tenths__

   d.   9 tenths + 9 tenths = __18 tenths = 1 and 8 tenths__

Example 1.

   Add: 7 + 3.6 + 5.8

$7 + 3.6 + 5.8 = 16.4$

Discussion

   You can, of course, add horizontally as it is presented.

   •   6 tenths + 8 tenths = 14 tenths

       14 tenths = 4 tenths and 1

   •   1 + 7 + 3 + 5 = 16

Example 2.

   Add: 7.8 + 13 + 2.9

Discussion:

   You can also add vertically, but as you set the numbers in their
appropriate columns, you have to be sure that all tenths are
in the tenths column, and the ones are in the ones column.
You can rewrite 13 as 13.0. Complete the work.

$$\begin{array}{r} 7.8 \\ 13.0 \\ +\ 2.9 \\ \hline 23.7 \end{array}$$

EXERCISES

1. Add and then use a decimal point to write the answer:

a.

Ones	Tenths
	35
	7
1	3

= __1.3__

b.

Ones	Tenths
6	8
2	7
9	5

= __9.5__

c.

Tens	Ones	Tenths
	9	8
	4	6
1	4	4

= __14.4__

d.

Tens	Ones	Tenths
1	2	8
2	7	6
4	0	4

= __40.4__

2. Add:

a.	b.	c.	d.
3.5 + 2.9 **6.4**	26.3 + 51.9 **78.2**	34.6 + 5.7 **40.3**	25.4 + 14.6 **40.0**

e.	f.	g.	h.
7.6 4.2 + 9.8 **21.6**	2.9 7.6 + 8.4 **18.9**	32.4 6.8 + 57.9 **97.1**	80.5 3.7 + 15.8 **100.0**

i.	j.	k.	l.
17.8 70.1 64.9 + 9.2 **162.0**	8.1 135.9 2.6 + 24.4 **171.0**	49.2 261.8 39.0 + 100.9 **450.9**	7.8 19.4 29.6 + 113.2 **170.0**

3. Add:

a. $9.6 + 15.8$ = __25.4__   b. $13.4 + 2.6$ = __16.0__

c. $15 + 2.6 + 3.9 =$ __21.5__   d. $8.7 + 4.9 + 4$ = __17.6__

e. $17 + 2.9 + 4.8 =$ __24.7__   f. $7.8 + 6.9 + 0.4 =$ __15.1__

g. $2.8 + 3 + 9.6$ = __15.4__   h. $4.9 + 40 + 6$ = __50.9__

i. $1.7 + 30 + 9.1 =$ __40.8__   j. $9.6 + 4 + 8.8$ = __22.4__

k. $3.8 + 5 + 30.8 =$ __39.6__   l. $60 + 40.5 + 9.8 =$ __110.3__

13

6   SUBTRACTING

You know that:

8 tenths - 1 tenth = __7 tenths__

7 tenths - 7 tenths = __0 tenths__

Similarly:

a. 6 tenths - 5 tenths = __1 tenth__   b. 4 tenths - 0 tenths = __4 tenths__

c. 10 tenths - 4 tenths = __6 tenths__   d. 10 tenths - 9 tenths = __1 tenth__

e. 13 tenths - 8 tenths = __5 tenths__   f. 12 tenths - 4 tenths = __8 tenths__

Example 1.

Cities A, B, and C lie on the same road.

The distance from A to C is 9 miles.

The distance from A to B is 5.4 miles.

How far is B from C?

A •————————————————• B ————————— • C

Discussion:

To find the required distance we have to subtract 5.4 from 9.

- There are no tenths to subtract from.

    We change one (from the 9 ones) into 10 tenths.

    10 tenths - 4 tenths = 6 tenths

- 8 ones - 5 ones = 3 ones

$$\begin{array}{r} 9.0 \\ - 5.4 \\ \hline 3.6 \end{array}$$

Example 2.

Subtract: 9.1 - 5.4

Discussion:

- There are not enough tenths from which to subtract 4 tenths.

    You exchange 1 (from the 9 ones) for 10 tenths.

    Now you have 11 tenths.

    11 tenths - 4 tenths = 7 tenths

- 8 ones - 5 ones = 3 ones

$$\begin{array}{r} 9.1 \\ - 5.4 \\ \hline 3.7 \end{array}$$

Note:

When you subtract vertically, make sure that the tenths are in the same column, the ones are in the same column, the tens are in the same column, ... etc.

Also, the decimal points have to be in the same column.

EXERCISES

1. Subtract and then use a decimal point to write the answer:

a.

Tens	Ones	Tenths
5	6	4
2	7	8
2	8	6

= __28.6__

b.

Tens	Ones	Tenths
4	7	1
4	6	9
0	0	2

= __0.2__

2. Subtract:

a.
```
    9.6
  - 2.3
    7.3
```

b.
```
    6.0
  - 3.7
    2.3
```

c.
```
    9.0
  - 3.2
    5.8
```

d.
```
    8.1
  - 7.4
    0.7
```

e.
```
    4.2
  - 3.8
    0.4
```

f.
```
   19.4
  - 7.8
   11.6
```

g.
```
   27.3
  - 19.5
    7.8
```

h.
```
   30.5
  - 23.8
    6.7
```

3. Subtract:

a. 9.2 - 3.8 = __5.4__

b. 18.1 - 8.7 = __9.4__

c. 36.5 - 14.8 = __21.7__

d. 70.3 - 18.6 = __51.7__

e. 4 - 2.1 = __1.9__

f. 7 - 3.2 = __3.8__

APPLICATIONS

1. The distance to school is 3 miles.
You walked 1.7 miles and then got a ride to school.
How long was the distance you rode?   3.0 - 1.7 = 1.3 miles

2. A, B, C and D are four bus stops.
AD is 10 miles, AB is 2.8 miles, and BC
is 3.9 miles. How far is C from D?

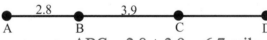

a. ABC = 2.8 + 3.9 = 6.7 miles
b. CD = 10.0 - 6.7 = 3.3 miles

3. The difference between two numbers is 7.9.
The larger number is 16.
What is the other number?   16.0 - 7.9 = 8.1

4. The difference between two numbers is 6.4.
The smaller number is 8.8.
What is the other number?   8.8 + 6.4 = 15.2

5. The sum of N and 8.9 is 12.7.
What number is N?   N = 12.7 - 8.9 = 3.8

Date _____

7 MULTIPLYING BY TENS, HUNDREDS OR THOUSANDS

Study the chart below:

1000's	100's	Tens	Ones	Tenths
			9	4

- If you move any digit one place to the left, its new value will be 10 times its original value.
- If you move any digit two places to the left, its new value will be 100 times its original value.
- If you move each digit one place to the left, the new number you obtain will be 10 times the original number.
- If you move each digit two places to the left, the new number you obtain will be 100 times the original number.

You can, of course, use a decimal point instead of the chart.

- If you move the decimal point one place to the right, the number you obtain will be 10 times the original number, $10 \times 9.4 = 94$
which is the same as multiplying the number by 10.
- If you move the decimal point two places to the right, the number you obtain will be 100 times the original number,
$100 \times 9.4 = 940$
which is the same as miltiplying the number by 100.
- If you move the decimal point three places to the right, the number you obtain will be 1000 times the original number, $1000 \times 9.4 = 9400$
which is the same as multiplying the number by 1000.

EXERCISES

Write the answer:

a. 10×4.8 =   48

b. 10×6.9 =   69

c. 10×7.2 =   72

d. 10×15.3 =   153

e. $10 \times .9$ =   9

f. 10×29.4 =   294

g. 100×3.2 =   320

h. 100×6.8 =   680

i. 100×1.7 =   170

j. 100×4.9 =   490

k. 1000×12.9 =   12900

l. 1000×25.8 =   25800

m. 1000×3.9 =   3900

n. 1000×5.8 =   5800

MULTIPLYING BY A ONE DIGIT NUMERAL

You know that
- a.   3 x 2 tenths = 6 tenths
- b.   2 x 4 tenths = _8 tenths_
- c.   4 x 2 tenths = _8 tenths_
- d.   3 x 3 tenths = _9 tenths_

You also know that:
- e.   6 x 4 tenths = 24 tenths = 2 ones and 4 tenths
- f.   7 x 5 tenths = _35 tenths = 3 ones and 5 tenths_
- g.   8 x 7 tenths = _56 tenths = 5 ones and 6 tenths_

Example 1.
Multiply: 7 x 2.6

Tens	Ones	Tenths
1	8	2

7 x 2.6 =

- •   7 x 6 tenths = 42 tenths = 4 ones and 2 tenths
  Write 2 in the tenths place and remember that you
  have 4 ones to add to the ones you obtain later.   7 x 2.6 = _18.2_
- •   7 x 2 ones = 14 ones
  14 ones + 4 ones = 18 ones = 1 ten and 8 ones
  Write 8 in the ones place and 1 in the tens place.

EXERCISES

1. Multiply and then use a decimal point to write the answer:

a.   8 x 1.4 =

Tens	Ones	Tenths
1	1	2

= _11.2_

b.   5 x 4.8 =

Tens	Ones	Tenths
2	4	0

= _24.0_

c.   6 x 3.2 =

Tens	Ones	Tenths
1	9	2

= _19.2_

d.   7 x 4.3 =

Tens	Ones	Tenths
3	0	1

= _30.1_

2. Multiply:

- a. 4 x 2.5   = _10.0_
- b. 8 x 3.6   = _28.8_
- c. 3 x 11.8 = _35.4_
- d. 9 x 14.7 = _132.3_
- e. 6 x 7.5   = _45.0_
- f. 9 x 4.5   = _40.5_
- g. 2 x 14.6 = _29.2_
- h. 5 x 3.7   = _18.5_
- i. 6 x 26.4 = _158.4_
- j. 7 x 9.6   = _67.2_
- k. 4 x 107.6 = _430.4_
- l. 5 x 14.8 = _74.0_

m.
```
    9.7
  x 8
   77.6
```

n.
```
   14.2
  x  3
   42.6
```

o.
```
    25.8
  x  7
  180.6
```

p.
```
   13.5
  x  6
   81.0
```

q.
```
    8.5
  x 4
   34.0
```

r.
```
   17.6
  x  4
   70.4
```

s.
```
    29.8
  x  5
  149.0
```

t.
```
  112.5
  x   8
  900.0
```

Date _____

8 MULTIPLYING BY TENS, HUNDREDS OR THOUSANDS

Example 1.

To get the answer to 20 x 4.7, you can follow one of two methods.

a. • Multiply 4.7 by 10.   10 x 4.7 = 47
   • Multiply the answer by 2.   20 x 4.7 = 2 x 47 = 94
b. • Change 4.7 into 47 tenths.
   • Multiply: 20 x 47.   20 x 47 = 940
   • The answer is in tenths.
     Change 940 tenths into 94.0. 20 x 47 = 94.0

Example 2.

To get the answer to 300 x 2.9, you can do the following:

• Change 2.9 into 29 tenths.
• Multiply 29 by 300.   300 x 29 = 8700
• The answer is in tenths.
  Change into ones, tens, and hundreds.   300 x 2.9 = 870.0

Example 3.

Multiply: 4000 x 1.8

Discussion:

• Multiply 4000 x 18.   4000 x 18 = 72000
• This answer is in tenths.   4000 x 1.8 = 7200.0
  Write the answer in the standard form.

EXERCISES

1. Multiply:
   a. 30 x 5.7   = __171.0__   b. 70 x 8.4   = __588.0__
   c. 90 x 1.6   = __144.0__   d. 50 x 4.4   = __220.0__
   e. 800 x 3.8 = __3040.0__   f. 600 x 1.7 = __1020.0__
   g. 900 x 4.2 = __3780.0__   h. 700 x 2.6 = __1820.0__
   i. 2000 x 6.2 = __12400.0__   j. 9000 x 1.2 = __10800.0__
   k. 4000 x 2.7 = __10800.0__   l. 5000 x 3.4 = __17000.0__

2. Find the answer:
   a. 900 - (30 x 9.7)   b. (20 x 9.8) + (200 x 1.3)

   __900 - 291.0 = 609__   __196.0 + 260.0 = 456.0__

MULTIPLYING BY TWO OR THREE-DIGIT NUMERALS

Example 1.
24 x 3.8 may be carried out in two different ways.

a. 4 x 3.8 = __15.2__
  20 x 3.8 = __76.0__
  Add   = __91.2__

b. Change 3.8 into 38 tenths.
  24 x 38 tenths = 912 tenths
  912 tenths = 91.2

$$\begin{array}{r} 38 \\ \times\ 24 \\ \hline 152 \\ 76 \\ \hline 912 \end{array}$$

Example 2.
Multiply: 37 x 2.6 both ways.

a. 7 x 2.6 = __18.2__
  30 x 2.6 = __78.0__
  37 x 2.6 = __96.2__

b. Change 2.6 into 26 tenths.
  37 x 26 tenths = 962 tenths
  962 tenths = __96.2__

$$\begin{array}{r} 37 \\ \times\ 26 \\ \hline 222 \\ 74 \\ \hline 962 \end{array}$$

The second method is more frequently used than the first.

EXERCISES

Multiply:

a. 76 x 1.2 = 91.2	b. 39 x 2.1 = 81.9	c. 63 x 2.4 = 151.2
d. 48 x 3.9 = 187.2	e. 95 x 1.4 = 133	f. 285 x 3.6 = 1026
g. 105 x 1.6 = 168	h. 170 x 3.5 = 595	i. 150 x 2.5 = 375

19

EXERCISES

1. Write the answer:
   a. 10 x 34.5   = 345
   b. 10 x 20.6   = 206
   c. 100 x 34.5 = 3450
   d. 100 x 20.6 = 2060
   e. 1000 x 34.5 = 34500
   f. 1000 x 20.6 = 20600
   g. 100 x 3.8   = 380
   h. 10 x 245.6 = 2456
   i. 10 x 14.9   = 149
   j. 1000 x 2.7 = 2700

2. Multiply:
   a. 600 x 2.7   = 1620.0
   b. 40 x 29.1   = 1164.0
   c. 60 x 2.7   = 162.0
   d. 4000 x 29.1 = 116400.0
   e. 6000 x 2.7 = 16200.0
   f. 400 x 29.1 = 11640.0
   g. 700 x 3.9   = 2730.0
   h. 80 x 13.1   = 1048.0

3. Multiply:
   a. 7 x 14.9 = 104.3
   b. 3 x 45.9 = 137.7
   c. 5 x 4.7   = 23.5
   d. 4 x 9.8   = 39.2
   e. 9 x 25.2 = 226.8
   f. 6 x 36.8 = 220.8
   g. 8 x 2.5   = 20.0
   h. 5 x 25.2 = 126.0

4. Multiply:

a. 38.4 x 7 = 268.8	b. 91.6 x 4 = 366.4	c. 35.7 x 6 = 214.2	d. 47.5 x 9 = 427.5
e. 30.2 x 4 = 120.8	f. 24.5 x 6 = 147.0	g. 24.3 x 7 = 170.1	h. 27.5 x 8 = 220.0

5. Multiply:

a. 23 x 6.5 = 149.5	b. 85 x 34.6 = 2941.0	c. 125 x 1.8 = 225.0
d. 76 x 14.1 = 1071.6	e. 29 x 23.1 = 669.9	f. 34 x 2.8 = 95.2

APPLICATIONS

1. Tom covers 15.8 miles on 1 gallon of gas.
   What distance does he cover on 19 gallons?   19 x 15.8 = 300.2

2. The daily production of milk on a
   dairy farm fills 87 containers whose
   capacity is 8.5 gallons each. How many
   gallons is the daily production of milk?   87 x 8.5 = 739.5

3. A, B, and C are points on the map of a road.
   AC is 9 times as long as AB.
   AB represents 13.5 miles.
   How many miles are represented by BC?   9 x 13.5 = 121.5

A   B   C

4. What number do you add to (35 x 8.1)   (35 x 8.1) = 283.5
   for the answer to be 300?   N = 300 - 283.5 = 16.5

5. What number do you subtract from   92 x 9.1 = 837.2
   92 x 9.1 for the answer to be 15?   N = 837.2 - 15 = 822.2

6. X, Y, and Z are three numbers.
   X is 28.7, Y is 5 times X, and Z is 10 times Y.
   • What number is Y?   Y = 5 x 28.7 = 143.5
   • What number is Z?   Z = 10 x 143.5 = 1435

7. A = 26 x 3.7
   B = A - 25.7   A = 96.2
   What number is B?   B = 96.2 - 25.7 = 70.5

8. Find the answer:
   a. 70 - (25 x 1.7)   b. (30 x 1.4) + (50 x 3.4)

   70 - 42.5 = 27.5   42 + 170 = 212

Level 13

Date _____

Example 1.
    5 identical objects weigh 23.5 lb.
    How much does one object weigh?
Discussion:
    The situation calls for the division: $23.5 \div 5$.

$$\frac{04.7}{5)\,23.5}$$

    To do this division you do the following:
- 2 T's $\div$ 5 = 0 T's and 2 T's remain.
- 2 T's are changed into 20 ones.
   20 ones + 3 ones = 23 ones.
   23 ones $\div$ 5 = 4 ones and 3 ones remain.
- 3 ones are changed into 30 tenths.
   30 tenths + 5 tenths = 35 tenths.
   35 tenths $\div$ 5 = 7 tenths.

The answer is 4 and 7 tenths. The answer is 4.7 lb.

Example 2.
    The division to the right has not been completed.
    You have a remainder of 4 ones.

$$\frac{121.5}{8)\,972.0}$$

Discussion:
    You can continue the division by changing the 4 ones into 40 tenths.
    40 tenths $\div$ 8 = 5 tenths.   The answer is <u>121.5</u>

Example 3.
    Do the division to the right step by step.
- 3H's $\div$ 4 = 0H's and 3H's remain.

$$\frac{075.5}{4)\,302}$$

- 3H's are changed into 30 tens.
   30 $\div$ 4 = 7 tens and 2 tens remain.
- 2 tens are changed into 20 ones.
   20 ones + 2 ones = 22 ones.
   22 ones $\div$ 4 = 5 ones and 2 ones remain.
- 2 ones are changed into 20 tenths.
   20 tenths $\div$ 4 = 5 tenths.   The answer is <u>75.5</u>

Example 4.
    Complete the division: $\dfrac{025.9}{7)\,181.3}$

Example 5.
    Complete the division: $\dfrac{030.1}{5)\,150.5}$

EXERCISES

Divide:

a. $\dfrac{47.4}{2)\,94.8}$	b. $\dfrac{06.5}{5)\,32.5}$	c. $\dfrac{11.9}{6)\,71.4}$	d. $\dfrac{052.9}{5)\,264.5}$
e. $\dfrac{015.6}{8)\,124.8}$	f. $\dfrac{017.3}{9)\,155.7}$	g. $\dfrac{099.7}{3)\,299.1}$	h. $\dfrac{073.7}{4)\,294.8}$
i. $\dfrac{20.3}{3)\,60.9}$	j. $\dfrac{20.4}{4)\,81.6}$	k. $\dfrac{090.6}{8)\,724.8}$	l. $\dfrac{040.4}{6)\,242.4}$
m. $\dfrac{18.5}{4)\,74}$	n. $\dfrac{064.2}{5)\,321}$	o. $\dfrac{12.5}{6)\,75}$	p. $\dfrac{096.5}{8)\,772}$

APPLICATIONS

1. You travelled 72 miles on 5 gallons of gas.
   How many miles per gallon did your car go?   <u>14.4 miles</u> $\dfrac{14.4}{5)\,72.0}$

2. Sam made 18.2 pounds of jam.
   He filled 7 identical jars.
   How much jam did each jar hold?   <u>2.6 pounds</u> $\dfrac{02.6}{7)\,18.2}$

3. Dan had a rope 117.5 yards long.
   He divided it equally into 5 pieces.
   How long is each piece?   <u>23.5 yards</u> $\dfrac{023.5}{5)\,117.5}$

4. 6 times a number is 637.2.
   What is the number?   <u>106.2</u> $\dfrac{106.2}{6)\,637.2}$

5. Given that A is 197.4, and that
   A is 7 times B, what number is B?   <u>B = 197.4 ÷ 7 = 28.2</u>

6. Find the answer:
   a. (312.5 ÷ 5) - (3 x 6.9)

   62.5 - 20.7 = 41.8

   b. (3 x 128.4) ÷ 6

   385.2 ÷ 6 = 064.2

     Level 13

Example 6.
The division example to the right has not been completed.
- You have a remainder of 17.
- You change 17 ones into 170 tenths
  and then add 5 tenths you have.
  So, you have 175 tenths.
  175 tenths divided by 25 = 7 tenths.
  The answer is __38.7__ .

```
       038.7
   25) 967.5
       75
       217
       200
        17.5
        17.5
```

Example 7.
The division example to the right has not been completed.
- You have a remainder of 12 ones.
- You change 12 ones into 120 tenths.
  120 tenths divided by 24 = __5 tenths__ .
  The answer is __15.5__ .

```
       015.5
   24) 372
       24
       132
       120
        12 0
        12 0
```

EXERCISES

Divide:

a.
```
       035.7
   20) 714.0
       60
       114
       100
        140
        140
```

b.
```
       030.2
   30) 906.0
       90
       060
        60
```

c.
```
       023.6
   14) 330.4
       28
       50
       42
        84
        84
```

d.
```
       0103.2
   28) 2889.6
       28
       089
        84
         56
         56
```

e.
```
       011.3
   25) 282.5
       25
       32
       25
        75
        75
```

f.
```
       013.5
   27) 364.5
       27
       94
       81
       135
       135
```

g.
```
       014.8
   16) 236.8
       16
       76
       64
       128
       128
```

h.
```
       040.8
   15) 612.0
       60
       120
       120
```

i.
```
       003.8
   65) 247.0
       195
       520
       520
```

j.
```
       007.8
   79) 616.2
       553
       632
       632
```

k.
```
       060.4
   15) 906.0
       90
       060
        60
```

l.
```
       0005.7
   176) 1003.2
        880
        1232
        1232
```

APPLICATIONS

1. 25 parcels of the same weight
    weigh 357.7 pounds.
    Find the weight of one parcel. $357.5 \div 25 = 14.3$ lb.

2. You travelled 106.4 miles at a
    speed of 19 miles per hour.
    How much time did you take? $106.4 \div 19 = 5.6$ hours

3. Sue had a ribbon 16.1 yards long.
    She used the ribbon to make 23 identical bows.
    How much ribbon did each bow take? $16.1 \div 23 = 0.7$ yards

4. A dozen eggs weighed 25.2 ounces.
    Assuming that the eggs are of the same
    weight, what is the weight of one egg? $25.2 \div 12 = 2.1$ ounces

5. If you work steadily, you can mow
    1.5 acres in 3 hours.
    At the same rate, how many acres can   a. 1 hour: $1.5 \div 3 = 0.5$ acres
    you mow in 7 hours?   b. 7 hours: $7 \times 0.5 = 3.5$ acres

6. The product of two numbers is 91.2.
    One number is 38.
    What is the other number? $91.2 \div 38 = 2.4$

7. Find the answer: 8. Find the answer:
    $(79.5 \div 15) + (66.6 \div 37)$ $(25 \times 3.9) \div 13$
    a. $79.5 \div 15 = 5.3$ a. $25 \times 3.9 = 9.75$
    b. $66.6 \div 37 = 1.8$ b. $97.5 \div 13 = 7.5$
    c. $5.3 + 1.8 = 7.1$

9. X is 30×4.9 10. A is 32.5.
    $Y = X \div 35$ A is 25 times as large as B.
    What number is Y?   What number is B?
    $X = 147$ $B = 32.5 \div 25 = 1.3$
    $Y = 147 \div 35 = 4.2$

Level 13

UNIT A TEST

1. "1 third of the figure is shaded."
   What does this mean?
   The figure is divided into 3 equal parts,
   and 1 part is shaded.

   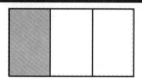

2. "2 fifths of the figure are shaded."
   What does this mean?
   The figure is divided into 5 equal parts,
   and 2 parts are shaded.

   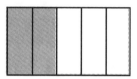

3. The figure is divided into equal parts. What fraction of the figure is shaded?

   a.    b.    c.

   $\frac{1}{10}$ $\frac{7}{100}$ $\frac{57}{100}$

4. Write the number that represents the following:
   a. 1 and 1 fifth $1\frac{1}{5}$ b. 3 and 1 tenth $3\frac{1}{10}$
   c. 8 and 2 thirds $8\frac{2}{3}$ d. 7 and 9 tenths $7\frac{9}{10}$
   e. $6 + \frac{3}{4}$ $6\frac{3}{4}$ f. $19 + \frac{23}{100}$ $19\frac{23}{100}$

5. a. Write how you would read the numeral 0.8   8 tenths
   b. Write how you would read the numeral 1.7   one and 7 tenths
   c. Use a decimal point to write $5\frac{3}{10}$ 5.3
   d. Use a decimal point to write $\frac{92}{10}$ 9.2

6. Write the number represented in the boxes:

   a.
Tens	Ones	Tenths
3	5	2
   = 35.2

   b.
Tens	Ones	Tenths
4		6
   = 40.6

7. Write the missing number:
   a. 8 = __80__ tenths   b. 5.8 = __58__ tenths   c. 39.7 = __397__ tenths

8. Write in the standard form:
   a. 7 tenths = __0.7__   b. 35 tenths = __3.5__   c. 250 tenths = __25__

9. Add:
   a. $2.9 + 6.4 + 8.5 =$ __17.8__
   b. $3.8 + 6.5 + 4.7 =$ __15.0__
   c. $3 + 2.9 + 6.8 \ \ =$ __12.7__
   d. $3.8 + 45 + 2.9 =$ __51.7__

   e.
   $$\begin{array}{r} 7.4 \\ 2.8 \\ 0.3 \\ + \ 10.6 \\ \hline 21.1 \end{array}$$

   f.
   $$\begin{array}{r} 5.4 \\ 6 \\ 8.9 \\ + \ 3.8 \\ \hline 24.1 \end{array}$$

   g.
   $$\begin{array}{r} 16.9 \\ 3.2 \\ 7.0 \\ + \ 4.9 \\ \hline 32.0 \end{array}$$

10. Subtract:
    a. $9.6 - 3.4 \ \ =$ __6.2__
    b. $25.2 - 8.9 =$ __16.3__
    c. $35 - 9.7 \ \ \ =$ __25.3__

    d.
    $$\begin{array}{r} 15.1 \\ - \ 7.8 \\ \hline 7.3 \end{array}$$

    e.
    $$\begin{array}{r} 70 \\ - \ 46.9 \\ \hline 23.1 \end{array}$$

    f.
    $$\begin{array}{r} 31.0 \\ - \ 23.4 \\ \hline 7.6 \end{array}$$

11. Multiply:
    a. $10 \times 0.8 \ \ =$ __8__
    b. $10 \times 3.7 \ \ =$ __37__
    c. $10 \times 10.9 \ =$ __109__
    d. $100 \times 0.7 =$ __70__
    e. $100 \times 1.9 =$ __190__
    f. $100 \times 30.6 =$ __3060__

12. Multiply:
    a. $3 \times 4.2 \ \ \ \ =$ __12.6__
    b. $7 \times 3.8 \ \ \ \ =$ __26.6__
    c. $8 \times 13.5 \ \ \ \ =$ __108.0__

13. Multiply:
    a. $40 \times 1.3 \ \ =$ __52.0__
    b. $70 \times 0.8 \ \ =$ __56.0__
    c. $50 \times 3.4 \ \ \ \ =$ __170.0__
    d. $300 \times 2.1 =$ __630.0__
    e. $200 \times 0.1 =$ __20.0__
    f. $600 \times 1.8 \ \ =$ __1080.0__

14. Multiply:

a. 43×1.8	b. 36×2.7	c. 28×3.5
__77.4__	__97.2__	__98.0__

15. Divide:

a. $\dfrac{07.9}{5)\,39.5}$	b. $\dfrac{20.9}{4)\,83.6}$	c. $\dfrac{1.8}{5)\,9}$
d. $25)\,\overline{87.5}$ $\begin{array}{r}03.5\\ \hline \ \ 75\\ \hline 125\\ 125\\ \hline\end{array}$	e. $18)\,\overline{365.4}$ $\begin{array}{r}020.3\\ \hline 36\\ \hline \ \ 54\\ 54\\ \hline\end{array}$	f. $24)\,\overline{324}$ $\begin{array}{r}013.5\\ \hline 24\\ \hline 84\\ 72\\ \hline 120\end{array}$

16. You covered 124.8 miles on 8 gallons of gas. How many miles did you cover on 1 gallon? $124.8 \div 8 = 15.6$

17. 15 chocolate bars weigh 52.5 ounces. Assuming that the bars are of the same weight, find the weight of 7 bars.   7 bars: $7 \times 3.5 = 24.5$ oz.

10 HUNDREDTHS

B

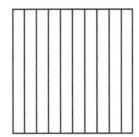

The whole is divided into 10 equal parts.
One part is 1 tenth of the whole.

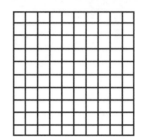

Each one-tenth of the whole is divided into equal parts.
Each part is 1 hundredth of the whole.

The figure is divided into equal parts.
What fraction of the figure is shaded?

a.

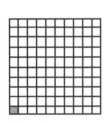

1 hundredth

b.

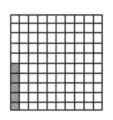

5 hundredths

c.

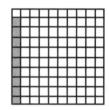

9 hundredths

d.

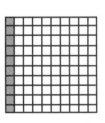

10 hundredths

e.

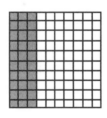

30 hundredths

f.

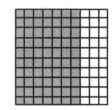

70 hundredths

g.

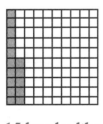

15 hundredths

h.

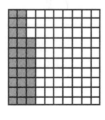

27 hundredths

i.

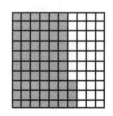

63 hundredths

The "hundredth" fits into our system of writing numbers. We can add a new box for the "hundredths" to the right of that for the "tenths".

Hundreds	Tens	Ones	Tenths	Hundredths

The same system of grouping and exchanging applies to the hundredths.

- 10 hundredths are grouped into 1 tenth.
- 1 tenth may be exchanged for 10 hundredths.

Examples:

- The numeral to the right is read "3 hundredths". Using the decimal point, this numeral is written .03 or 0.03.

Ones	10th's	100th's
		3

- The numeral to the right is read "15 hundredths". It is written 0.15.

Ones	10th's	100th's
	1	5

- The number presented in the boxes to the right has to be rewritten. Using a decimal point, we write it in the standard form.

Ones	10th's	100th's
6	1	38

is written

6	4	8	= 6.48

APPLICATIONS

Do the grouping required and rewrite the number.

a.

Ones	10th's	100th's
		27

should be rewritten

	2	7	= 0.27

b.

Ones	10th's	100th's
4	7	38

should be rewritten

5	0	8	= 5.08

c.

10's	Ones	10th's	100th's
	9	8	26

should be rewritten

1	0	0	6	= 10.06

d.

10's	Ones	10th's	100th's
8	0	70	45

should be rewritten

8	7	4	5	= 87.45

e.

10's	Ones	10th's	100th's
3	7	35	37

should be rewritten

4	0	8	7	= 40.87

f.

10's	Ones	10th's	100th's
	16	35	80

should be rewritten

2	0	3	0	= 20.30

ONE CENT IS 1 HUNDREDTH OF ONE DOLLAR

One of the most familiar applications for "hundredths" is to express an amount of money in dollars (which includes cents).

You know that 100 cents are equivalent to 1 dollar.

Thus: 1 cent = $\$\frac{1}{100}$ = \$0.01

Example 1.

    Express in dollars the amount of money pictured to the right.

Discussion:

    The amount is 9 cents.

    The amount is 9-hundreths of 1 dollar.

    The amount is \$0.09.

Example 2.

    Express in dollars the amount of money pictured to the right.

Discussion:

    The amount is 28 cents.

    The amount is 28-hundredths of a 1 dollar.

    The amount is \$0.28.

Example 3.

    Express in dollars the amount of money pictured to the right.

Solution:

    The amount is 2 dollars and 76 cents.

    The amount is \$2.76.

Example 4.

    You have 3 five-dollar bills and 8 dimes.

    How much money do you have?

Solution:

    The amount is 15 dollars and 80 cents.

    The amount is \$15.80.

APPLICATIONS

Express in dollars the amounts of money pictured below:

a.  <u>$2.15</u>	b.  <u>$0.08</u>	c.  <u>$12.10</u>
d. <u>$0.12</u>	e. <u>$1.06</u>	f.  <u>$5.25</u>

2. In dollars, how much is each amount?
    a.   2 five-dollar bills and 9 dimes   <u>$10.90</u>
    b.   1 ten-dollar bill, 3 one-dollar bills and 15 nickels   <u>$13.75</u>
    c.   6 one-dollar bills, 3 dimes, and 7 nickels   <u>$6.65</u>
    d.   1 twenty-dollar bill and 8 pennies   <u>$20.08</u>
    e.   1 ten-dollar bill and 5 dimes   <u>$10.50</u>
    f.   2 one-hundred bills and 6 pennies   <u>$200.06</u>
    g.   9 quarters   <u>$2.25</u>
    h.   14 nickels   <u>$0.70</u>

3. In dollars, how much is each amount?
    a.   7¢   = <u>$0.07</u>   b.   19¢   = <u>$0.19</u>
    c. $1 and 30¢ = <u>$1.30</u>   d. $8 and 35¢   = <u>$8.35</u>
    e.   90¢   = <u>$0.90</u>   f. $2 and 4¢   = <u>$2.04</u>
    g. $1 and 1¢ = <u>$1.01</u>   h. $100 and 1¢ = <u>$100.01</u>

Level 13

11 ADDING AND SUBTRACTING

Example 1.

    You bought a book for $3.98, and
a note-book for $1.75.

    How much did you pay?

Discussion:

    The situation calls for the addition: 3.98 + 1.75

    You may use boxes as shown to the right.

	Ones	10th's	100th's
	3	9	8
+	1	7	5
=	4	16	13
=	**5**	**7**	**3**

- Add hundreths to hundredths, tenths to tenths,
  ones to ones, … etc.

- If needed, group hundreds to tenths, tenths to ones, … etc.

You can also use the decimal point and do the grouping as you carry

out the process, step by step, as follows: 3.98 + 1.75 = 5.73

- 8 hundredths + 5 hundredths = 13 hundredths.
  13 hundredths is grouped into 1 tenth and 3 hundredths.
  Write 3 in the hundredths place, and remember that you
  have 1 tenth to add to the tenths.

- 1 tenth + 9 tenths + 7 tenths = 17 tenths.
  17 tenths is grouped into 1 and 7 tenths.
  Write 7 in the tenths place and remember that you have 1 to add
  to the ones.

- To separate the fractions from wholes write the decimal point.

- 1 + 3 + 1 = 5 $3.98 + $1.75 = **$5.73**   You pay **$5.73**

Example 2.

    You had $6.42. You spent $2.97.   6.42

    How much did you have left?   - 2.97

Discussion: 3.45

    It is obvious that you have to subtract: 6.42 - 2.97

    If you study the situation, you find that you have to exchange
1 tenth for 10 hundredths, and 1 for 10 tenths.

- 12 hundredths - 7 hundredths = 5 hundredths.

- 13 tenths - 9 tenths = 4 tenths.

- 5 ones - 2 ones = 3 ones.

    The amount left was: **$3.45**

1. Add:

a.
10's	Ones	10th's	100th's
	6	3	5
+	5	8	9
= 1	2	2	4

b.
10's	Ones	10th's	100th's
	7	6	4	2
+	9	5	8
= 8	6	0	0

c.   13.98
   + 17.07
   31.05

d.   36.57
   + 1.74
   38.31

e.   12.90
   + 1.46
   14.36

f.   7.04
   + 8.90
   15.94

g. 9.84 + 0.62 = ___10.46___

h. 0.97 + 0.74 = ___1.71___

i. 7.69 + 2.3 = ___9.99___

j. 7.87 + 9.14 = ___17.01___

k. 19.46 + 2.08 + 0.05 = ___21.59___

l. 7.46 + 8.4 + 6.09 = ___21.95___

2. Subtract:

a.
10's	Ones	10th's	100th's
	7	5	8
+	6	4	9
= 1	0	9	

b.
10's	Ones	10th's	100th's
	9	6	2	4
-	5	3	7	6
= 4	2	4	8

c.   53.38
   - 8.19
   45.19

d.   37.07
   - 4.38
   32.69

e.   80.00
   - 7.96
   72.04

f.   64.45
   - 9.55
   54.90

g. 70.94 - 14.68 = ___56.26___

h. 47.07 - 6.42 = ___40.65___

i. 97.04 - 28.96 = ___68.08___

j. 60. - 4.94 = ___55.06___

k. 56.09 - 17.90 = ___38.19___

l. 48. - 19.47 = ___28.63___

3. Find the answer:

a. Add 16.98 to 3.75 and subtract
   the answer from 50.

   • 16.98 + 3.75 = 20.73
   • 50.00 - 20.73 = 29.27

b. Subtract 6.89 from 8.2 and add
   the answer to 17.69.

   • 8.20 - 6.89 = 1.31
   • 17.69 + 1.31 = 19.00

c. Add the sum of 19.38 and 4.76 to
   the difference between 20 and 7.1.

   • 19.98 + 4.76 = 24.74
   • 20.00 - 7.10 = 12.90
                    37.64

12 MULTIPLYING BY TENS, HUNDREDS OR THOUSANDS

Study the chart shown below:

1000's	100's	10's	Ones	10ths	100ths
			9	4	5

- If you move any digit one place to the left, its new value will be 10 times its original value.
- If you move any digit two places to the left, its new value will be 100 times its original value.
- If you move each digit one place to the left, the new number you obtain will be 10 times the original number.
- If you move each digit two places to the left, the new number you obtain will be 100 times the original number.

You can, of course, use a decimal point instead of the chart.

- If you move the decimal point one place to the right, the number you obtain will be 10 times the original number, which is the same as multiplying the number by 10. $10 \times 9.45 = 94.5$
- If you move the decimal point two places to the right, the number you obtain will be 100 times the original number, which is the same as multiplying the number by 100. $100 \times 9.45 = 945$
- If you move the decimal point three places to the right, the number you obtain will be 1000 times the original number, which is the same as multiplying the number by 1000. $1000 \times 9.45 = 9450$

EXERCISES

Write the answer:

a. 10×3.75 = __37.5__   b. 10×9.08 = __90.8__

c. 10×0.76 = __7.6__   d. 10×0.03 = __0.3__

e. 10×23.92 = __239.2__   f. 10×20.05 = __200.5__

g. 100×6.92 = __692__   h. 100×3.07 = __307__

i. $100 \times .85$ = __85__   j. $100 \times .06$ = __6__

k. 1000×6.95 = __6950__   l. 1000×2.04 = __2040__

m. 1000×0.32 = __320.0__   n. 1000×0.01 = __10__

MULTIPLYING BY A ONE-DIGIT NUMERAL

Example 1.

Joan bought 4 yards of fabric at $2.39 a yard.

How much did she pay (excluding tax)?

Discussion:

It is obvious that the required amount is 4 x 2.39 dollars.

- You can do the calculations using boxes.

Ones	10th's	100th's		Ones	10th's	100th's
8	12	36		9	5	6

$4 \times 2.39 = $ | = 9.56

- You also can do the computation in one step by doing the grouping (into tenths, ones … etc.) mentally.

Ones	10th's	100th's
9	5	6

$4 \times 2.39 = $ | = 9.56

You can also do the computation using the decimal point, as shown below.

a. 9 x 1.05 = 9.45   b. 5 x 1.02 = 5.10   c. 8 x 4.85 =   38.80

EXERCISES

1. Multiply:

a. 6 x 4.89   = 29.34   b. 7 x 18.09 = 126.63

c. 9 x 15.92 = 143.28   d. 8 x 24 .16 = 193.28

e. 5 x 3.85 = 19.25   f. 8 x 12.65 = 101.20

g. 3 x 8.76 = 26.28   h. 7 x 25.34 = 177.38

i. 2 x 23.05 = 46.10   j. 4 x 42.05 = 168.20

2. Find the answer:

a. (6 x 9.56) + (3 x 14.29)   57.36 + 42.87 = 100.23

b. X = 30 - (7 x 3.05)

What number is X?   X = 30 - 21.35 = 8.65

c. B = 3 x (9 x 1.84)

What number is B?   B = 3 x 16.56 = 49.68

Level 13

13 MULTIPLYING BY TENS, HUNDREDS OR THOUSANDS

Example 1.
Multiply 30 x 5.48
Discussion:
- You know that 5.48 = 548 hundredths
- Multiply: 30 x 548   30 x 548 = 16440
  The answer is in hundredths.
- Use the decimal point to write the answer
  in the standard form which is hundredths,   30 x 5.48 = 164.40
  tenths, ones, … etc.

Example 2.
Given that 50 x 123 = 6150,
you can conclude that 50 x 1.23 = 61.50

Example 3.
Given that 800 x 245 = 196000,
you can conclude that 800 x 2.45 = 1960.00

EXERCISES

1. Multiply:
   - a. 50 x 1.26 = __63.00__
   - b. 40 x 2.64 = __105.60__
   - c. 80 x 2.78 = __222.40__
   - d. 60 x 0.94 = __56.40__
   - e. 30 x 9.61 = __288.30__
   - f. 20 x 4.31 = __86.20__
   - g. 40 x 4.05 = __162.00__
   - h. 50 x 3.08 = __154.00__
   - i. 60 x 1.25 = __75.00__
   - j. 80 x 0.05 = __4.00__

2. Find the answer:
   - a. (80 x 1.24) - 35.96   99.20 - 35.96 = 63.24
   - b. 7.98 - (30 x 0.05)   7.89 - 1.50 = 6.48
   - c. (50 x 1.24) - (30 x 0.75)   62.00 - 22.50 = 39.50
   - d. (60 x 0.03) + (90 x 0.01)   1.80 + 0.90 = 2.70
   - e. (20 x 1.09) + (30 x 0.06)   21.80 + 1.80 = 23.60
   - f. (10 x 23.87) + (50 x 4.04)   238.70 + 202.00 = 440.70
   - g. (60 x 3.05) - (100 x 1.16)   183.00 - 116 = 67.00

MULTIPLYING BY TWO OR THREE-DIGIT NUMERALS

Example 1.

Multiply: 25 x 3.19

Discussion:

- You know that 3.19 = 319 hundredths

Multiply 25 x 319

The answer is 7975 hundredths.

Use the decimal point to write the answer
in the standard form which is hundredths,
tenths, ones, … etc.

$$
\begin{array}{r}
319 \\
\times\ 25 \\
\hline
1595 \\
638 \\
\hline
7975
\end{array}
$$

25 x 3.19 = __79.75__

Example 2.

Given that 38 x 194 = 7372

you can conclude that 38 x 1.94 = __73.72__

EXERCISES

1. Multiply:

a. 84 x 1.52	b. 38 x 5.16	c. 79 x 1.04
__127.68__	__196.08__	__82.16__
d. 95 x 1.07	e. 105 x 1.05	f. 901 x 1.09
__101.65__	__110.25__	__982.09__

2. Find the answer:

a. 200 - (35 x 2.16)

__200 - 75.6 = 124.4__

b. (28 x 2.45) - (26 x 1.25)

__68.6 - 32.5 = 36.1__

B

14 DIVIDING BY A WHOLE NUMBER

Example 1.
  Divide 7.48 ÷ 4

$$\frac{1.87}{4)\,7.48}$$

Discussion:

  Do the work step by step:

  • 7 ones ÷ 4 = 1, 3 ones remain.

  • 34 tenths ÷ 4 = 8 tenths, 2 tenths remain.

  • 28 hundreds ÷ 4 = 7 hundredths   The answer is **1.87**

B

Example 2.
  Divide 81.75 ÷ 25

$$\begin{array}{r} 03.27 \\ 25)\overline{81.75} \\ \underline{75} \\ 67 \\ \underline{50} \\ 175 \\ \underline{175} \end{array}$$

Discussion:

  Do the work step by step:

  • 8 tens ÷ 25 = 0 tens, 8 tens remain.

  • 81 ones ÷ 25 = 3 ones, 6 ones remain.

  • 67 tenths ÷ 25 = 2 tenths, 17 tenths remain.

  • 175 hundredths ÷ 25 = 7 hundredths   The answer is **3.27**

Example 3.
  Divide 64.05 ÷ 21

$$\begin{array}{r} 03.05 \\ 21)\overline{64.05} \\ \underline{63} \\ 105 \\ \underline{105} \end{array}$$

Discussion:

  Do the work step by step:

  • 6 tens ÷ 21 = 0 tens, 6 tens remain.

  • 64 ones ÷ 21 = 3 ones, 1 remains.

  • 10 tenths ÷ 21 = 0 tenths, 10 tenths remain.

  • 105 hundredths ÷ 21 = 5 hundredths   The answer is **3.05**

Example 4.
Complete the work:
  You have to change the tenths that remain into hundredths.

$$\begin{array}{r} 02.35 \\ 38)\overline{89.30} \\ \underline{76} \\ 133 \\ \underline{114} \\ 190 \\ \underline{190} \end{array}$$

Example 5.
Complete the work:
  You have to change the ones that remain into tenths, and the tenths that remain into hundredths.

$$\begin{array}{r} 01.25 \\ 36)\overline{45.00} \\ \underline{36} \\ 90 \\ \underline{72} \\ 180 \\ \underline{180} \end{array}$$

38

Divide:

a. $\dfrac{1.23}{8)\,9.84}$	b. $\dfrac{0.77}{5)\,3.85}$	c. $\dfrac{1.05}{7)\,7.35}$	d. $\dfrac{0.65}{6)\,3.90}$
e. $\dfrac{0.06}{9)\,0.54}$	f. $\dfrac{2.03}{3)\,6.09}$	g. $\dfrac{1.55}{4)\,6.20}$	h. $\dfrac{0.95}{8)\,7.60}$

i.
$$
\begin{array}{r}
00.56 \\
26)\,\overline{14.56} \\
\underline{13\,0} \\
1\,56 \\
\underline{1\,56}
\end{array}
$$

j.
$$
\begin{array}{r}
01.05 \\
38)\,\overline{39.90} \\
\underline{38} \\
1\,90 \\
\underline{1\,90}
\end{array}
$$

k.
$$
\begin{array}{r}
010.05 \\
15)\,\overline{150.75} \\
\underline{15} \\
0\,75 \\
\underline{75}
\end{array}
$$

l.
$$
\begin{array}{r}
01.04 \\
25)\,\overline{26.00} \\
\underline{25} \\
100 \\
\underline{100}
\end{array}
$$

m.
$$
\begin{array}{r}
03.01 \\
24)\,\overline{72.24} \\
\underline{72} \\
24 \\
\underline{24} \\
00
\end{array}
$$

n.
$$
\begin{array}{r}
02.05 \\
34)\,\overline{69.70} \\
\underline{68} \\
1\,70 \\
\underline{1\,70} \\
0\,00
\end{array}
$$

o.
$$
\begin{array}{r}
01.35 \\
24)\,\overline{32.40} \\
\underline{24} \\
8\,4 \\
\underline{7\,2} \\
1\,20 \\
\underline{1\,20}
\end{array}
$$

p.
$$
\begin{array}{r}
01.25 \\
36)\,\overline{45.00} \\
\underline{36} \\
9\,0 \\
\underline{7\,2} \\
1\,80 \\
\underline{1\,80}
\end{array}
$$

APPLICATIONS

1. You bought 24 cartons of orange juice.
   You paid $33.36.
   How much was the price of 1 carton? $33.36 ÷ 24 = $1.39

2. You had one 20-dollar bill.
   You bought 5 pounds of meat.
   You had $8.55 left.   a. 20.00 - 8.51 = 11.45
   How much was the price of 1 lb. of meat?   b. $11.45 ÷ 5 = $2.29

3. Miss Jones bought 26 copies of a book.
   She paid $84.50.
   If she returns 3 books, how much money   a. $84.50 ÷ 26 = $3.25
   does she get back?   b. 3 x 3.25 = $9.75

4. The price of 14 pounds of apples at
   $0.39 a pound is the same as the price
   of 6 pounds of grapes.   a. 14 x $0.39 = $5.46
   Find the price of grapes per pound.   b. $5.46 ÷ 6 = $0.91

B

Level 13

APPLICATIONS

1. The tank of your car has a capacity of 15 gallons.
   With a full tank you can drive 273.75 miles.
   How far can you go on 1 gallon of gas? $273.75 \div 15 = 18.25$ miles

2. You consume 100 gallons of gas monthly.
   If the average price is $1.29, how much
   do you monthly pay for gas? $100 \times \$1.29 = \$129.00$

3. Dick earns $3.75 per hour.
   He worked for 35 hours.
   How much was his total earnings? $35 \times \$3.75 = \$131.25$

4. Joe saves $3.25 weekly.
   How much are Joe's savings in a year?
   (The year is 52 weeks). $52 \times \$3.25 = \$169.00$

5. You had $20.
   You bought 4 notebooks for $1.69 each.   a. $4 \times \$1.69 = \$6.76$
   You paid sales tax of 54¢.   b. $\$6.76 + \$0.54 = \$7.30$
   How much did you have left?   c. $\$20.00 - \$7.30 = \$12.70$

6. You had 37 quarters.   a. $37 \times \$0.25 = \$9.25$
   Now you have 9 dimes and 8 nickels.   b. $90¢ + 40¢ = 130¢ = \$1.30$
   How much did you spend?   c. $\$9.25 - \$1.30 = \$7.95$

7. You had one 20-dollar bill. You bought   a. $10 \times \$1.09 = \$10.90$
   10 cans of fruit for $1.09 each, and   b. $3 \times \$2.39 = \$7.17$
   3 pounds of meat at $2.39 per pound.   c. $\$10.90 + \$7.17 = \$18.07$
   How much did you have left?   d. $\$20.00 - \$18.07 = \$1.93$

8. a. What number do you add to 7.98
for the answer to be 15.01? $15.01 - 7.98 = 7.03$

b. What number do you subtract from
15.01 for the answer to be 7.98? $15.01 - 7.98 = 7.03$

9. a. The sum of two numbers is 3.05.
One of the numbers is 0.97.
What is the other number? $3.05 - 0.97 = 2.08$

b. The difference between two numbers is 1.97.
The smaller number is 8.06.
What is the other number? $8.06 + 1.97 = 10.03$

c. The difference between two numbers is 2.85.
The larger number is 7.16.
What is the other number? $7.16 - 2.85 = 4.31$

10. a. You multiplied a number by 25.
The answer was 3.75.
What was the number? $3.75 \div 25 = 0.15$

b. You divided a number by 28.
The answer was 1.07.
What was the number? $28 \times 1.07 = 29.96$

11. You started with a number.
You added 3.97 and then multiplied by 5.
The answer was 28.25.   a. $28.25 \div 5 = 5.65$
What was the number you started with?   b. $5.65 - 3.97 = 1.68$

12. You started with a number.
You divided by 24, and then multiplied by 8.
The answer was 5.04.   a. $5.04 \div 8 = 0.63$
What was the number you started with?   b. $24 \times 0.63 = 15.12$

13. A + (25 x 1.27) = 39.02   a. $25 \times 1.27 = 31.75$
What number is A?   b. $A = 39.02 - 31.75 = 7.27$

14. X + (100 x 3.09) = 605   a. $X + 309 = 605$
What number is X?   b. $X = 605 - 309 = 296$

Level 13

Date _____

1. Use a decimal point to write the number presented in the boxes:

a.
10's	Ones	10th's	100th's
5	2	6	38
= **52.98**

b.
10's	Ones	10th's	100th's
	8	14	61
= **10.01**

2. Write the numerals you read:
   a. Sixty and thirty-seven hundredths   **60.37**
   b. Nine and five hundredths   **9.05**
   c. Forty and 3 hundredths   **40.03**

3. Is the equation "3.8 = 3.80" correct?   **Yes**
   Why?   **1 tenth = 10 hundredths**
                         8 tenths = 80 hundredths

4. Express in dollars:

   a.   **$0.27**
   b.    **$1.05**
   c.    **$10.35**

   d. 7 one dollar bills and 2 dimes   **$7.20**
   e. 1 ten dollar bill and 1 nickel   **$10.05**

5. Add:
   a. 7.35 + 8.96   = **16.31**   b. 5.8 + 4.69 + 7.05   = **17.54**
   c. 2.06 + 9 + 1.8 = **12.86**   d. 6 + 3.7 + 9.56 + 4.1 = **23.36**

   e.   10.50   f.   9.35   g.   3.03   h.   6.95
            3   3.0   0.90   7.08
       + 7.94   + 2.47   + 1.48   + 0.70
         21.44   14.82   5.41   14.73

6. Subtract:
   a. 49.87 - 8.75 = **41.12**   b. 34.51 - 7.96 = **26.55**
   c. 6.79 - 6.4   = **0.39**   d. 7 - 3.73   = **3.27**

   e.   9.67   f.   25.3   g.   30.0   h.   90.05
        - 3.8   - 16.79   - 14.76   - 23.97
           5.87   8.51   15.24   66.08

B

7. Multiply:
   a. 4 x 2.12 = __8.48__
   b. 5 x 4.63 = __23.15__
   c. 8 x 3.85 = __30.80__
   d. 7 x 1.43 = __10.01__

   e.   2.13
   $$\begin{array}{r} 2.13 \\ \times\ \ 3 \\ \hline 6.39 \end{array}$$

   f.   1.98
   $$\begin{array}{r} 1.98 \\ \times\ \ 7 \\ \hline 13.86 \end{array}$$

   g.   8.03
   $$\begin{array}{r} 8.03 \\ \times\ \ 6 \\ \hline 48.18 \end{array}$$

   h.   2.25
   $$\begin{array}{r} 2.25 \\ \times\ \ 4 \\ \hline 9.00 \end{array}$$

8. Multiply:
   a. 10 x 3.58   = __35.8__
   b. 100 x 8.69   = __869__
   c. 1,000 x 6.07 = __6070__

9. Multiply:
   a. 30 x 0.78   = __23.40__
   b. 400 x 2.05   = __820.00__
   c. 7,000 x 0.09 = __630.00__

10. Multiply:
    a. 25 x 8.26 = __206.50__
    b. 37 x 9.38 = __347.06__
    c. 125 x 0.24 = __30.00__

11. Divide:
    a.
    $$\begin{array}{r} 01.64 \\ 8\overline{)13.12} \end{array}$$

    b.
    $$\begin{array}{r} 03.61 \\ 5\overline{)18.05} \end{array}$$

    c.
    $$\begin{array}{r} 20.05 \\ 4\overline{)80.20} \end{array}$$

    d.
    $$\begin{array}{r} 0.15 \\ 25\overline{)3.75} \\ \underline{25} \\ 125 \\ \underline{125} \end{array}$$

    e.
    $$\begin{array}{r} 03.05 \\ 24\overline{)73.20} \\ \underline{72} \\ 1\,20 \\ \underline{1\,20} \end{array}$$

    f.
    $$\begin{array}{r} 0.25 \\ 18\overline{)4.50} \\ \underline{3\,6} \\ 90 \\ \underline{90} \end{array}$$

12. You bought meat for $3.69 and 15 cans of fruit. You paid $15.54. Assuming that the cans were of the same price, find the price of 1 can.

    a. $15.54 - $3.69 = $11.85
    b. $11.85 ÷ 15 = $0.79

13. You had 2 ten-dollar bills. You bought 5 notebooks for $ 1.39 each. How much did you have left?

    a. 5 x $1.39 = $6.95
    b. $20.00 - $6.95 = $13.05

14. Find the answer:
    a. (10 x 3.56) + (8 x 1.25)
    b. (70.5 ÷ 5) - (4 x 2.36)

    a. 35.6 + 10.00 = 45.6
    b. 14.10 - 9.44 = 4.66

Level 13

B

Date _____

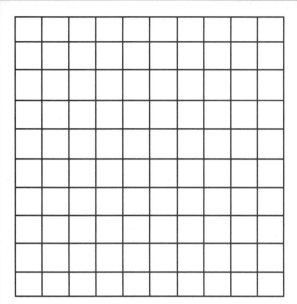

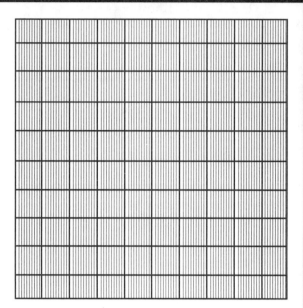

You are familiar with this figure.
The whole is divided into 100 equal parts.
Each part is one-hundredth of the whole.

Each 1-hundredth is divided into 10 equal parts.
The whole is divided into 1000 equal parts.
Each part is 1-thousandth of the whole.

Remember:

    10 thousandths are grouped into 1 hundredth.

    1 hundredth is exchanged for 10 thousandths.

With this important property, a new box for the "thousandths" is added to the right of the "hundredths".

Ones	10ths	100ths	1000ths

The numeral to the right is read "3 thousandths". Using the decimal point this numeral is written .003 or 0.003.

Ones	10ths	100ths	1000ths
	0	0	3

This numeral is read "25 thousandths", and is written 0.025.

Ones	10ths	100ths	1000ths
	0	2	5

This numeral is read "769 thousandths", and is written 0.769

Ones	10ths	100ths	1000ths
	7	6	9

GROUPING AND EXCHANGING

Example 1.
   How many thousandths are in: a. 7 hundredths   b. 6 tenths   c. 9 ones
Discussion:
   a. 1 hundredth = 10 thousandths   7 hundredths = _70 thousandths_
   b. 1 tenth = 10 hundredths = 100 thousandths   6 tenths   = _600 thousandths_
   c. 1 = 1000 thousandths   9 ones   = _9000 thousandths_

Example 2.
   The number presented in the boxes to the right
   has to be rewritten using a decimal
   point and in the standard form.

Ones	10ths	100ths	1000ths
5	17	24	38

is written

Ones	10ths	100ths	1000ths
6	9	7	8

= _6.978_

APPLICATIONS

1. Use a decimal point to write the numeral presented in the boxes:

a.
Ones	10ths	100ths	1000ths
	2	3	8

= _0.238_

b.
Ones	10ths	100ths	1000ths
		5	4

= _0.054_

c.
Ones	10ths	100ths	1000ths
			9

= _0.009_

d.
Ones	10ths	100ths	1000ths
			67

= _0.067_

e.
Ones	10ths	100ths	1000ths
		5	48

= _0.098_

f.
Ones	10ths	100ths	1000ths
8	3	24	7

= _8.547_

2. Write the numerals which you read as follows: (Use the decimal point)
   a. 6 and 235 thousandths   _6.235_   b. 14 and 7 thousandths   _14.007_
   c. 9 and 28 thousandths   _9.028_   d. 80 and 1 thousandth   _80.001_

3. Answer the following questions:
   a. How many hundredths are in 50 thousandths?   _5_
   b. How many thousandths are in 8 hundredths?   _80_
   c. How many thousandths are in 3 ones?   _3000_
   d. How many thousandths are in 6 tenths?   _600_
   e. How many thousandths are in 100?   _100,000_

Level 13

16 ADDING AND SUBTRACTING

Example 1:

Do the addition to the right:

Ones	10ths	100ths	1000ths
2	3	5	6
+ 4	2	3	8
= 6	5	9	4

- 6 thousandths + 8 thousandths = 14 thousandths
  14 thousandths = 4 thousandths and 1 hundredth
- 1 hundredth + 5 hundredths + 3 hundredths = 9 hundredths
- Now you can complete the work.

Example 2:

Do the subtraction to the right:

Ones	10ths	100ths	1000ths
9	6	3	2
- 5	8	4	7
= 3	7	8	5

Discussion:

- You cannot subtract 7 thousandths from 2 thousandths.
  You exchange 1 hundredth for 10 thousandths and add them to the 2 thousandths.
- 12 thousandths - 7 thousandths
- Now you can complete the work.

You can, of course, use the decimal point instead of the boxes.

- In the addition to the right, grouping is carried out.
  8 thousandths + 9 thousandths = 17 thousandths
- 17 thousandths are grouped into 1 hundredth and 7 thousandths

$$\begin{array}{r} 3.068 \\ + 2.759 \\ \hline 5.827 \end{array}$$

- In the subtraction to the right, exchanging is carried out.
  3 hundredths are exchanged for 2 hundredths and 10 thousandths.

$$\begin{array}{r} 6.837 \\ - 2.509 \\ \hline 4.328 \end{array}$$

- In the subtraction to the right, you have to write 9.1 as 9.100. The number has not changed because 1 tenth is the same as 100 thousandths.

$$\begin{array}{r} 9.100 \\ - 4.873 \\ \hline 4.227 \end{array}$$

Do the following additions and subtractions:

2.356 + 4.238 = __6.594__

9.632 - 5.847 = __3.785__

$$\begin{array}{r} 2.043 \\ + 1.821 \\ \hline 3.864 \end{array} \qquad \begin{array}{r} 2.356 \\ + 4.238 \\ \hline 6.594 \end{array} \qquad \begin{array}{r} 9.632 \\ - 5.847 \\ \hline 3.785 \end{array} \qquad \begin{array}{r} 4.502 \\ - 2.368 \\ \hline 2.134 \end{array}$$

1. Add:
   a. $3.859 + 2.764 =$ __6.623__
   b. $19.005 + 3.876 =$ __22.881__
   c. $8.448 + 3.255 =$ __11.703__
   d. $28.004 + 7.641 =$ __35.645__
   e. $4.894 + 3.008 + 6.47 =$ __14.372__
   f. $19.087 + 26.964 + 8.7 =$ __54.751__

   g. $\begin{array}{r} 3.851 \\ 4.139 \\ +\ 6.8 \\ \hline \mathbf{14.790} \end{array}$
   h. $\begin{array}{r} 18.059 \\ 1.63 \\ +\ 4.008 \\ \hline \mathbf{23.697} \end{array}$
   i. $\begin{array}{r} 70.849 \\ 9.165 \\ +\ 18.484 \\ \hline \mathbf{98.498} \end{array}$
   j. $\begin{array}{r} 25.195 \\ 16.846 \\ +\ 27.759 \\ \hline \mathbf{69.800} \end{array}$

2. Subtract:
   a. $35.9 - 7.618 =$ __28.282__
   b. $29.146 - 7.828 =$ __21.318__
   c. $37.854 - 8.68 =$ __29.174__
   d. $10.75 - 8.348 =$ __2.402__
   e. $28.8 - 13.951 =$ __14.849__
   f. $25.05 - 3.984 =$ __21.066__

   g. $\begin{array}{r} 9.648 \\ -\ 4.157 \\ \hline \mathbf{5.491} \end{array}$
   h. $\begin{array}{r} 16.409 \\ -\ 7.285 \\ \hline \mathbf{9.124} \end{array}$
   i. $\begin{array}{r} 28.6 \\ -\ 17.381 \\ \hline \mathbf{11.219} \end{array}$
   j. $\begin{array}{r} 10. \\ -\ 4.867 \\ \hline \mathbf{5.133} \end{array}$

APPLICATIONS

1. a. What number do you add to 3.009 for the answer to be 8?

   $8.000 - 3.009 = 4.991$

   b. What number do to you subtract from 8 for the answer to be 3.009?

   $8.000 - 3.009 = 4.991$

2. a. The sum of 5.968 and N is 9.127. What number is N?

   $N = 9.127 - 5.968 = 3.159$

   b. The difference between 7.682 and a larger number X is 3.06. What number is X?

   $X = 7.682 + 3.06 = 10.742$

   c. The difference between 7.682 and a smaller number Y is 3.06. What number is Y?

   $Y = 7.682 - 3.06 = 4.622$

17 MULTIPLYING BY TENS, HUNDREDS OR THOUSANDS

Study the chart shown below:

1000's	100's	10's	Ones	10ths	100ths
		3	6	9	4

- If you move any digit one place to the left, its new value will be 10 times its original value.
- If you move any digit two places to the left, its new value will be 100 times its original value.
- If you move each digit one place to the left, the new number you obtain will be 10 times the original number.
- If you move each digit two places to the left, the new number you obtain will be 100 times the original number.

You can, of course, use a decimal point instead of the chart.

- If you move the decimal point one place to the right, the number you obtain will be 10 times the original number, which is the same as multiplying the number by 10.

  $10 \times 3.694 = \underline{36.94}$

- If you move the decimal point two places to the right, the number you obtain will be 100 times the original number, which is the same as multiplying the number by 100.

  $100 \times 3.694 = \underline{369.4}$

- If you move the decimal point three places to the right, the number you obtain will be 1000 times the original number, which is the same as multiplying the number by 1000.

  $1000 \times 3.694 = \underline{3694}$

EXERCISES

Write the answer:

a. $10 \times 8.469 = \underline{84.69}$ b. $10 \times 7.609 = \underline{76.09}$

c. $10 \times 9.014 = \underline{90.14}$ d. $10 \times 6.007 = \underline{60.07}$

e. $100 \times 3.459 = \underline{345.9}$ f. $100 \times 8.091 = \underline{809.1}$

g. $100 \times 4.78 = \underline{478}$ h. $100 \times 7.005 = \underline{700.5}$

i. $1000 \times .092 = \underline{92}$ j. $1000 \times 6.093 = \underline{6093}$

k. $1000 \times 19.64 = \underline{19640}$ l. $1000 \times 6.005 = \underline{6005}$

Example 1.

To find the answer to 7 x 1.394:

Ones	10ths	100ths	1000ths
9	7	5	8

7 x 1.394 = (table above) = 9.758

- 7 x 4 thousandths = 28 thousandths
  28 thousandths = 8 thousandths and 2 hundredths
- 7 x 9 hundredths = 63 hundredths
  63 hundredths + 2 hundredths = 65 hundredths
  65 hundredths = 6 tenths and 5 hundredths
- 7 x 3 tenths = 21 tenths
  21 tenths + 6 tenths = 27 tenths
  27 tenths = 2 ones and 7 tenths
- 7 x 1 = 7
  7 + 2 = 9

You can, of course, use the decimal point instead of the boxes.

Do the following examples.

a. 7 x 1.394 = <u>9.758</u>

b. 8 x 5.014 = <u>40.112</u>

c. 5 x 3.024 = <u>15.120</u>

d.
```
  2.003
x     9
 18.027
```

e.
```
  0.769
x     3
  2.307
```

f.
```
  3.125
x     8
 25.000
```

Multiply:

a. 6 x 1.894 = <u>11.364</u>

b. 4 x 12.718 = <u>50.872</u>

c. 9 x 2.145 = <u>19.305</u>

d. 3 x 29.126 = <u>87.378</u>

e. 7 x 13.694 = <u>95.858</u>

f. 5 x 4.217 = <u>21.085</u>

g. 8 x 1.315 = <u>10.520</u>

h. 5 x 12.356 = <u>61.780</u>

i. 2 x 3.245 = <u>6.490</u>

j. 8 x 3.275 = <u>26.200</u>

k. 4 x 1.225 = <u>4.900</u>

l. 6 x 5.095 = <u>30.570</u>

m. 5 x 2.014 = <u>10.070</u>

n. 8 x 3.005 = <u>24.040</u>

o. 6 x 3.005 = <u>18.030</u>

p. 7 x 8.001 = <u>56.007</u>

18 MULTIPLYING BY TENS, HUNDREDS OR THOUSANDS

Example 1.

　　Multiply: 70 x 1.265

Discussion:

- Change 1.265 into thousandths　　　1.265 = 1265 thousandths
- Multiply: 70 x 1265　　　　　　　　70 x 1265 = 88550
- The answer is 88550 thousandths

　　Change it into the standard form: 88550 thousandths = 88.550

Example 2.

　　Multiply: 400 x 3.658

Solution:

- 3.658 = 3658 thousandths
- 400 x 3658 thousandths = 1463200 thousandths = 1463.200

EXERCISES

Multiply:

1. a. 30 x 7.812 = _234.360_　　　　b. 90 x 0.423 = _38.070_
　 c. 60 x 0.013 = _0.780_　　　　　 d. 60 x 5.023 = _301.380_
　 e. 70 x 3.006 = _210.420_　　　　 f. 90 x 4.102 = _369.180_
　 g. 50 x 1.368 = _68.400_　　　　　h. 60 x 2.035 = _122.100_
　 i. 40 x 3.905 = _156.200_　　　　 j. 80 x 0.015 = _1.200_

2. a. 200 x 1.637 = _327.400_　　　　b. 700 x 0.006 = _4.200_
　 c. 600 x 1.008 = _604.800_　　　　d. 500 x 5.056 = _2528.000_
　 e. 900 x 0.023 = _20.700_　　　　 f. 400 x 2.035 = _814.000_
　 g. 800 x 1.035 = _828.000_　　　　h. 300 x 0.904 = _271.200_
　 i. 500 x 0.208 = _104.000_　　　　j. 600 x 4.005 = _2403.000_

Find the answer:

　 a. (70 x 3.863) + (20 x 1.009)　　　_270.410 + 20.180 = 290.590_
　 b. (1000 x 9.007) - (400 x 9.468)　 _9007.000 - 3787.200 = 5219.800_
　 c. (600 x 3.874) - (500 x 2.34)　　 _2324.400 - 1170.000 = 1154.400_

MULTIPLYING BY TWO OR THREE-DIGIT NUMERAL'S

Example 1.

Multiply: 27 x 3.008

Discussion:

You may use one of two methods:

- 7 x 3.008 = **21.056** or • Change 3.008 into 3008 thousandths
- 20 x 3.008 = **60.160** • Multiply: 27 x 3008 thousandths, as shown.
- Add   81.216   • Write the answer in the standard form.

```
  3008
x   27
 21056
  6016
 81216
```

The second method is more frequently used than the first.

Example 2.	Example 3.
39 x 1274 = 49686	48 x 2125 = 102000
39 x 1.274 = **49.686**	48 x 2.125 = **102.000**

EXERCISES

1. Multiply:

a. 26 x 6.421	b. 38 x 3.015	c. 89 x 1.035
166.946	114.57	92.115
d. 56 x 0.425	e. 59 x 7.001	f. 364 x 2.025
23.800	413.059	737.100

2. Find the answer:

a. (24 x 1.005) - 0.127	b. (38 x 1.258) + (2.487 x 6)
24.120 - 0.127 = 23.993	47.804 + 14.922 = 62.726

19 DIVIDING BY A WHOLE NUMBER

Example 1.

Do the division to the right.

$$\frac{2.394}{4)\,9.576}$$

- 9 ones ÷ 4 = 2 ones, 1 remains
- 15 tenths ÷ 4 = 3 tenths, 3 tenths remain.
- 37 hundredths ÷ 4 = 9 hundredths, 1 hundredth remains.
- 16 thousandths ÷ 4 = 4 thousandths   The answer is 2.394

Example 2.

- 8 tenths ÷ 6 = 1 tenth, 2 tenths remain.
- 27 hundredths ÷ 6 = 4 hundredths, 3 hundredths remain.

$$\frac{0.145}{6)\,0.870}$$

- 30 thousandths ÷ 6 = 5 thousandths   The answer is 0.145

Example 3.

- 5 ones ÷ 8 = 0 ones, 5 ones remain.
- 50 tenths ÷ 8 tenths, 2 tenths remain.

$$\frac{0.625}{8)\,5.000}$$

- 20 hundredths ÷ 8 = 2 hundredths, 4 hundredths remain.
- 40 thousandths ÷ 8 = 5 thousandths   The answer is 0.625

EXERCISES

Divide:

a. $\frac{03.145}{5)\,15.725}$	b. $\frac{2.026}{4)\,8.104}$	c. $\frac{05.042}{3)\,15.126}$	d. $\frac{1.901}{5)\,9.505}$
e. $\frac{0.149}{7)\,1.043}$	f. $\frac{08.88}{8)\,71.04}$	g. $\frac{0.315}{6)\,1.890}$	h. $\frac{0.325}{4)\,1.300}$
i. $\frac{1.125}{8)\,9.000}$	j. $\frac{3.044}{3)\,9.132}$	k. $\frac{0.402}{9)\,3.618}$	l. $\frac{.061}{7)\,.427}$
m. $\frac{0.125}{8)\,1.000}$	n. $\frac{0.175}{4)\,0.700}$	o. $\frac{0.105}{4)\,0.420}$	p. $\frac{1.005}{7)\,7.035}$
q. $\frac{0.002}{6)\,0.012}$	r. $\frac{0.507}{6)\,3.042}$	s. $\frac{0.303}{4)\,1.212}$	t. $\frac{0.112}{9)\,1.008}$

Example 4.

- 6 tens ÷ 25 = 0 tens and a remainder of 6 tens.
- 65 ones ÷ 25 = 2 ones and a remainder of 15 ones.
- 152 tenths ÷ 25 = 6 tenths and a remainder of 2 tenths.
- 27 hundredths ÷ 25 = 1 hundredth and a remainder of 2 hundredths.
- 25 thousandths ÷ 25 = 1 thousandths.

```
        2.611
  25)65.275
     50
     152
     150
       27
       25
       25
       25
```

EXERCISES

Divide:

a.
```
       0.325
  25) 8.125
      7 5
       62
       50
       25
       25
```

b.
```
       02.047
  24) 49.128
      48
      1 12
        96
       168
       168
```

c.
```
       0.125
  38) 4.750
      3.8
       95
       76
      190
      190
```

d.
```
       0.132
  24) 3.168
      2 4
       76
       72
       48
       48
```

e.
```
       0.196
  25) 4.9
      2 5
      2 40
      2 25
       150
       150
```

f.
```
       00.875
  64) 56.000
      51 2
       4 80
       4 48
        320
        320
```

g.
```
       01.008
  75) 75.600
      75
       600
       600
```

h.
```
       0.109
  67) 7.303
      6 7
       603
       603
```

i.
```
        00.152
  125) 19.000
       12 5
        6 50
        6 25
         250
         250
```

j.
```
        00.401
  215) 86.215
       86 0
        215
        215
```

k.
```
        0.015
  624) 9.360
       6 24
       3 120
       3 120
```

l.
```
       00.303
  45) 13.635
      13 5
        135
        135
```

Level 13

20 DIVIDING BY TENS, HUNDREDS OR THOUSANDS

Study the chart shown below:

10's	Ones	10ths	100ths	1000ths
5	6	4		

You know that:

- If you move any digit one place to the right, its value becomes 1-tenth its original value.
- If you move each digit one place to the right, the new number you obtain will be 1-tenth the original number.
- If you move any digit two places to the right, its value becomes 1-hundredth its original value.
- If you move each digit two places to the right, the new number you obtain will be 1-hundredth the original number.
- If you move a digit three places to the right, its value becomes 1-thousandth its original value.
- If you move each digit three places to the right, the new number you obtain will be 1-thousandth the original number.

You may use a decimal point instead of the chart:

- If you move the decimal point one place to the left, the new number you obtain will be 1-tenth the original number, which is the same as dividing the number by 10. $56.4 \div 10 = 5.64$
- If you move the decimal point two places to the left, the new number you obtain will be 1-hundredth the original number, which is the same as dividing the number by 100. $56.4 \div 100 = 0.564$

Examples:

1. a. $9.78 \div 10 = \underline{0.978}$ b. $289.1 \div 100 = \underline{2.891}$

   c. $24.6 \div 10 = \underline{2.46}$ d. $17.8 \div 100 = \underline{0.178}$

   e. $378.2 \div 100 = \underline{3.782}$ f. $34.62 \div 10 = \underline{3.462}$

   g. $90.4 \div 10 = \underline{9.04}$ h. $100.06 \div 10 = \underline{10.006}$

   i. $0.8 \div 10 = \underline{0.08}$ j. $0.9 \div 100 = \underline{0.009}$

   k. $0.07 \div 10 = \underline{0.007}$ l. $0.1 \div 100 = \underline{0.001}$

Write the answer:
1. a. $78.9 \div 10 = \underline{7.89}$ b. $0.98 \div 10 = \underline{0.098}$
    c. $716.89 \div 10 = \underline{71.89}$ d. $0.01 \div 10 = \underline{0.001}$
    e. $56.2 \div 10 = \underline{5.62}$ f. $2.09 \div 10 = \underline{0.209}$

2. a. $167.3 \div 100 = \underline{1.673}$ b. $0.8 \div 100 = \underline{0.008}$
    c. $25.1 \div 100 = \underline{0.251}$ d. $1.2 \div 100 = \underline{0.012}$
    e. $789 \div 100 = \underline{7.89}$ f. $74 \div 100 = \underline{0.74}$

3. a. $1267 \div 1000 = \underline{1.267}$ b. $307 \div 1000 = \underline{0.307}$
    c. $29 \div 1000 = \underline{0.029}$ d. $1 \div 1000 = \underline{0.001}$
    e. $2816 \div 1000 = \underline{2.816}$ f. $817 \div 1000 = \underline{0.817}$

4. a. $978 \div 10 = \underline{97.8}$ 5. a. $7526 \div 10 = \underline{752.6}$
    b. $978 \div 100 = \underline{9.78}$ b. $7526 \div 100 = \underline{75.26}$
    c. $978 \div 1000 = \underline{0.978}$ c. $7526 \div 1000 = \underline{7.526}$

APPLICATIONS

1. 100 identical boxes weigh 35.9 kilograms.
    Find the weight of each box.
    $35.9 \div 100 = .359$ kilograms

2. 10 sheets of paper weigh 15.8 grams.
    Find the weight of one sheet.
    $15.8 \div 10 = 1.58$ grams

3. 100 paper clips weigh 85.1 grams.
    Find the weight of one paper clip.
    $85.1 \div 100 = 0.851$ grams

4. You covered 254.6 miles on 10 gallons of gas.
    How is your car on gas?
    $254.6 \div 10 = 25.46$ miles per gallon

5. Mary bought 100 yards of ribbon for $4.50.
    Sue bought 35 yards of the same ribbon
    for $1.89.
    Who had a better deal?
    Mary: $\$4.50 \div 100 = \$0.045$ per yard
    Sue: $\$1.89 \div 35 = \$0.054$ per yard
    Mary had a better deal.

APPLICATIONS

1. a. What number do you add to 7.841
      for the answer to be 10.295? — $\underline{10.295 - 7.841 = 2.454}$

   b. What number do you subtract from
      10.295 for the answer to be 7.841? — $\underline{10.295 - 7.841 = 2.454}$

2. a. You added a number to 3.896.
      The answer was 16.004.
      What was the number? — $\underline{16.004 - 3.896 = 12.108}$

   b. You added 3.896 to a number.
      The answer was 16.004.
      What was the number? — $\underline{16.004 - 3.896 = 12.108}$

3. a. You subtracted a number from 10.953.
      The answer was 4.006.
      What was the number? — $\underline{10.953 - 4.006 = 6.947}$

   b. You subtracted 10.953 from a number.
      The answer was 4.006.
      What was the number? — $\underline{10.953 + 4.006 = 14.959}$

4. a. The sum of two numbers is 15.806.
      The first number is 7.364.
      What is the second number? — $\underline{15.806 - 7.364 = 8.442}$

   b. The sum of two numbers is 15.806.
      The second number is 7.364.
      What is the first number? — $\underline{15.806 - 7.364 = 8.442}$

5. a. The difference between two numbers is
      5.897. The smaller number is 8.909.
      What is the other number? — $\underline{8.909 + 5.897 = 14.806}$

   b. The difference between two numbers is
      5.897. The larger number is 8.909.
      What is the other number? — $\underline{8.909 - 5.897 = 3.012}$

6. a. You multiplied a number by 8.
        The answer was 78.008.
        What was the number?   78.008 ÷ 8 = 09.751

    b. You divided a number by 8.
        The answer was 78.008.
        What was the number?   8 x 78.008 = 624.064

7. A + 7.564 = 12.009
    What number is A?   12.009 - 7.564 = 4.445

8. 9.865 + B = 15.873
    What number is B?   15.873 - 9.865 = 6.008

9. 2.004 - X = 1.926.
    What number is X?   2.004 - 1.926 = 0.078

10. Y - 3.705 = 6.263
    What number is Y?   6.263 + 3.705 = 9.968

11. A = 10 x 3.725
    B is 30 x A.
    What number is B?   B = 30 x 37.25 = 1117.50

12. X, Y and Z are three numbers.
    X is 0.903, Y is 10 x X
    and Z is 1 seventh of Y.   Y = 10 x 0.903 = 9.03
    What number is Z?   Z = 9.03 ÷ 7 = 1.29

13. You added 2.385 to a number, and
    then divided the answer by 6.
    The answer was 15.012.   a. 6 x 15.012 = 90.072
    What was the number?   b. 90.072 - 2.385 = 87.687

14. You multiplied a number by 7, and
    then subtracted 3.793.
    The answer was 18.096.   a. 18.096 + 3.793 = 21.889
    What was the number?   b. 21.889 ÷ 7 = 3.127

Level 13

21   MORE DECIMAL PLACES

We have worked with tenths, hundredths, and thousandths.

Ones	10ths	100ths	1000ths

If 1-1000th of a whole is divided into 10 equal parts, each part would be 1-10,000th of the whole. It means that ten 10,000ths may be grouped into one 1000th.

So, a new place for the 10,000ths may be added to the place system.

Ones	10ths	100ths	1000ths	10,000ths

If 1-10,000th of a whole is divided into 10 equal parts, each part would be 1-100,000th of the whole. It means that ten 100,000ths may be grouped into one 10,000th.

So, a new place for the 100,000ths may be added to the place system.

Ones	10ths	100ths	1000ths	10,000ths	100,000ths

Using the same principle, we can go on indefinitely, adding places to the right.

Ones	10ths	100ths	1000ths	10,000ths	100,000ths	1,000,000ths

EXERCISES

Study the numeral to the right.   93.7124085

   a. What does the 2 stand for?   1,000ths

   b. What does the 4 stand for?   10,000ths

   c. What does the 0 stand for?   100,000ths

   d. What does the 8 stand for?   1,000,000ths

   e. What does the 5 stand for?   10,000,000ths

   f. What digit is in the 10,000ths place?   4

   g. What digit is in the tens place?   9

   h. What digit is in the 1000ths place?   2

   i. What digit is in the millionths place?   8

MULTIPLYING AND DIVIDING BY 10s, 100s, 1,000s ... ETC.

Of special importance is multiplying and dividing a number with many decimal units by 10, 100, 1000, 10000, ... etc.

- If you follow the procedures you applied before you find:

$$10 \times 4.8947 = 48.947$$
$$100 \times 4.8947 = 489.47$$
$$1000 \times 4.8947 = 4894.7$$
$$10000 \times 4.8947 = 48947$$
$$100000 \times 4.8947 = 489470$$

- If you follow the procedures you used before you find:

$$18.46 \div 10 = 1.846$$
$$18.46 \div 100 = 0.1846$$
$$18.46 \div 1000 = 0.01846$$
$$18.46 \div 10000 = 0.001846$$
$$18.46 \div 100000 = 0.0001846$$

EXERCISES

1. Multiply:
   a. 10×7.4826 = __74.826__
   b. 100×9.7648 = __976.48__
   c. $1,000 \times 0.0948$ = __94.8__
   d. $10,000 \times 0.124865$ = __1248.65__
   e. $100,000 \times 2.4867$ = __248,670__
   f. $1,000 \times 394.42$ = __394,420__
   g. $27.8948 \times 1,000$ = __27,894.8__
   h. $3.9465 \times 1,000,000$ = __3,946,500__
   i. $10,000,000 \times 0.0094867$ = __94,867__
   j. $1,000,000 \times 3.760421$ = __3,760,421__

2. Divide:
   a. $19.4 \div 10$ = __1.94__
   b. $39.8 \div 100$ = __0.398__
   c. $76.1 \div 1,000$ = __0.0761__
   d. $84.6 \div 10,000$ = __0.00846__
   g. $2.4869 \div 100$ = __0.024869__
   h. $9104.62 \div 1,000$ = __9.10462__
   i. $309482 \div 1,000$ = __309.482__
   j. $29845 \div 100,000$ = __0.29845__

3. Find the answer:
   a. $(12748 \times 10000) + 30072.5$ $12748 + 30072.5 = 42820.5$
   b. $(70098 \div 1000) - 35.84$ $70.098 - 35.84 = 34.258$

    Level 13

EXERCISES

Please understand that accuracy is very important in the field of mathematics. If one digit is incorrect, or if the decimal point is in the wrong place, all your work is lost. Train yourself to be patient and accurate.

1. Add:

a. 39.72945	b. 7.64214	c. 16.0512	d. 0.78059
18.63149	0.0729	27.4934	0.31654
1.764	1.30516	30.0158	0.00421
0.3008	0.92148	9.7642	0.00096
60.42574	9.94168	83.3246	1.10230

e. 6.50694	f. 0.096487	g. 5.432098	h. 0.874231
0.076	1.2744	0.10608	1.90807
7.0098	5.008909	7.140688	0.443665
4.0607	4.00087	0.087605	2.053607
2.70653	1.065042	1.900764	7.000749
20.35997	11.445708	14.667235	12.280322

i. $37.5264 + 9.845 = $ _47.3714_   j. $5.864 + 9.00692 = $ _14.87092_

k. $8.0005 + 32.051 = $ _40.0515_   l. $.7694 + 5.816 = $ _6.5854_

m. $3.09784 + 0.7654 + 5.784 + 9.9724 = $ _19.61964_

n. $7.0643 + 3.0943 + 1.69004 + 1.00057 = $ _12.84921_

2. Subtract:

a. 74.8294	b. 7.96	c. 31.0091	d. 35
- 16.6129	- 4.8421	- 15.645	- 29.84216
58.2165	3.1179	15.3641	5.15784

e. 65.12004	f. 90.000003	g. 1.000031	h. 8.907050
- 48.90636	- 14.000439	- 0.900578	- 6.987694
16.21368	75.999564	0.099453	1.919356

i. $79.6458 - 64.76 = $ _14.8858_   j. $15.96 - 8.7481 = $ _7.2119_

k. $80 - 78.1254 = $ _1.8746_   l. $29.15 - 14.3619 = $ _14.7881_

m. $8.548275 - 7.79846 = $ _0.749815_   n. $10.29074 - 3.475358 = $ _6.815382_

o. $0.100001 - 0.000019 = $ _0.099982_   p. $3.010152 - 2.970573 = $ _0.039579_

3. Multiply:

a.	4.89467	b.	19.74684	c.	5.290068	d.	15.25125
	x 5		x 7		x 3		x 8
	24.47335		138.22788		15.870204		122.01000

e.	1.006548	f.	0.017805	g.	3.040706	h.	1.230801
	x 5		x 9		x 7		x 5
	5.032740		0.160245		21.284942		6.154005

i. 3 x 6.9845 = __20.9535__   j. 8 x 9.6125   = __76.9000__
k. 5 x 15.0006 = __75.0030__   l. 7 x 84.3756 = __590.6292__
m. 7 x 1.09703 = __7.67921__   n. 6 x 2.005635 = __12.033810__
o. 9 x 0.00046 = __0.00414__   p. 5 x 2.000018 = __10.000090__

q. 25 x 3.5786	89.4650	r. 48 x 1.80015	86.4072
s. 67 x 0.00018	0.01206	t. 56 x 0.1020104	5.7125824

4. Divide:

a.	__03.897249__	b.	__03.09531__	c.	__1.0002__	d.	__0.00021__
	5) 19.486245		8) 24.76248		7) 7.0014		9) 0.00189

e. __00.1006__
125) 12.5750
     12.5
       .0750
       .0750

f. __0.1075__
76) 8.17
    7.6
     .570
     .532
     .0380
     .0380

g. __01.5674__
26) 40.7524
    26
    14.7
    13.0
     1.75
     1.56
      .192
      .182
      .0104
      .0104

h. __006.37401__
37) 235.83837
    222
     13.8
     11.1
      2.73
      2.59
       .148
       .148
       .00037
       .00037

UNIT C TEST

1. a. Use the decimal point to write the number
   presented in the boxes to the right.
   b. What does one thousandth mean?

Ones	10ths	100ths	1000ths
9	3		8

   9.308

   One out of one thousand equal parts making 1 whole

2. a. How many thousandths are in 5.8?   5.8 = 5800 thousandths
   b. How many thousandths are in 0.79?   0.79 = 790 thousandths

3. a. Write 72 thousandths in the standard form.   .072
   b. Write 5682 thousandths in the standard form. 5.682

4. Add:

   a. $17.5 + 2.073 + 1.009 =$ 20.582

   b. $36 + 27.986 + 3.09 =$ 67.076

   c. $9.006 + 2.17 + 132 =$ 143.176

   d.   4.67
           5.199
        + 6.004
          15.873

   e.   29.86
           1.086
        + 2.7
          33.646

   f.   24.08
         126.857
        + 0.063
         151.000

5. Subtract:

   a. $29.815 - 13.986 =$ 15.829

   b. $30 - 24.876   =$ 5.124

   c. $84.24 - 3.009   =$ 81.231

   d.   14.654
       - 9.785
          4.869

   e.   28.41
       - 6.876
         21.534

   f.   19
       - 4.706
         14.294

6. Multiply:
   a. $10 \times 46.037 =$ 460.37
   b. $1000 \times 3.007 =$ 3007
   c. $100 \times 0.089 =$ 8.9

7. Multiply:
   a. $6 \times 1.004 =$ 6.024
   b. $9 \times 0.128 =$ 1.152
   c. $5 \times 12.018 =$ 60.090

8. Multiply:
   a. $40 \times 1.239 =$ 49.560
   b. $80 \times 0.015 =$ 1.200
   c. $300 \times 1.012 =$ 303.600
   d. $5000 \times 0.008 =$ 40.000

9. Multiply:
   a. 31×5.013 b. 123×1.804 c. 124×0.015

   = 155.403   = 221.892   = 1.860

10. Divide:

a.   05.216 / 7) 36.512

b.   05.925 / 8) 47.400

c.   0.625 / 8) 5.000

d.   03.251 / 18) 58.518

e.   0.054 / 29) 1.566

f.   0.125 / 24) 3.000

11. Write the answer:

a. $48 \div 10$ = __4.8__
b. $7.9 \div 10$ = __0.79__
c. $0.07 \div 10$ = __0.007__

d. $138 \div 100$ = __1.38__
e. $1.7 \div 100$ = __0.017__
f. $0.5 \div 100$ = __0.005__

g. $5238 \div 1000$ = __5.238__
h. $238 \div 1000$ = __0.238__
i. $25 \div 1000$ = __0.025__

12. In the number to the right:

9.0568747

a. What does 8 stand for?   __10,000ths__

b. What digit is in the millionths place? __4__

13. Write the answer:

a. 100×3.00908 = __300.908__
d. $67.89605 \div 100$ = __0.678905__

b. $10,000 \times 0.546703$ = __5467.03__
e. $4563.007 \div 1,000$ = __4.563007__

c. $1,000,000 \times 2.00008745$ = __2000087.45__
f. $2654.1 \div 100,000$ = __0.026541__

14. Find the answer:

a.   7.6421
    9.85648
+5.4096
  22.90818

b. 16.35
- 7.12942
  9.22058

c. 25.0071
- 12.3604
  12.6467

d. 23.
- 8.7296
  14.2704

e. 6×3.59264 = __21.55584__
f. 8×7.462515 = __59.700120__

g. 5×0.0908107 = __0.4540535__
h. 7×8.00102 = __56.00714__

15. Divide:

a.   01.1006 / 24) 26.4144
  24
  2.4
  2.4
    .0144
    .0144

b.   012.7004 / 39) 495.3156
  39
  105
   78
  27.3
  27.3
    .0156
    .0156

c.   00.30015 / 147) 44.12205
  44.1
  220
  147
  735
  735

D

22 THE METRIC SYSTEM OF MEASURES

In 1790, the French Academy of Sciences appointed a committee to devise a system of measures that would be easy to use. The committee invented what is known as the Metric System of Measures.

The United States of America is the only industrialized country which has not yet switched completely to the Metric System, but arrangements are being made towards this goal. As you shop and travel, you see signs and labels where metric units are used.

Basic Units:
As basic units, the committee adopted the "meter" for length, the "liter" for capacity, and the "gram for weight. The following table shows how basic Metric units and customary English units are related:

- 1 meter = 39.37 inches
  1 inch = 0.0254 meter

- 1 liter = 0.908 dry quart
  1 dry quart = 1.101 liters

- 1 gram = 0.035 ounce
  1 ounce = 28.35 grams

- 1 liter = 1.0576 liquid quarts
  1 liquid quart = 0.9464 liter

Using these relationships, you can work out other relationships:
- 1 foot = 12 inches = 12 x 0.254 meters = __0.3048__ meters
- 1 yard = 36 inches = 36 x 0.0254 meters = __0.9144__ meters

- 1 gallon = 4 quarts = 4 x 0.9464 liters = __3.7856__ liters
- 1 pint = $\frac{1}{2}$ liquid quart = 0.9464 liters ÷ 2 = __0.4732__ liters

- 1 pound = 16 ounces = 16 x 28.35 grams = __453.6__ grams

Larger and smaller units:
Using the decimal system of numeration, the committee derived larger and smaller units of measure:
- A unit which is 10 times the basic unit
- A unit which is 100 times the basic unit
- A unit which is 1000 times the basic unit
- A unit which is 1-tenth of the basic unit
- A unit which is 1-hundredth of the basic unit
- A unit which is 1-thousandth of the basic unit

The prefix system:

To identify the large and small units, the committee chose certain prefixes to be affixed to any of the three basic units

  a. For larger units:
  • Deca, to mean 10 times the basic unit
  • Hecto, to mean 100 times the basic unit
  • Kilo, to mean 1,000 times the basic unit

  b. For smaller units:
  • Deci, to mean 0.1 the basic unit
  • Centi, to mean 0.01 the basic unit
  • Milli, to mean 0.001 the basic unit

• The chart shows how the larger and smaller units are related to the basic unit.

KILO	HECTO	DECA	BASIC	DECI	CENTI	MILLI
1,000's	100's	10's	UNIT	10ths	100ths	1,000ths

• The chart is identical to the place-value chart you are familiar with.

1000's	100's	10's	ONES	10ths	100ths	1000ths

• Using the prefixes, you can fill the following table:

UNITS OF MEASURE	LENGTH	CAPACITY	WEIGHT
Basic unit	meter	liter	gram
10 x basic unit	decameter	decaliter	decagram
100 x basic unit	hectometer	hectoliter	hectogram
1,000 x basic unit	kilometer	kiloliter	kilogram
0.1 x basic unit	decimeter	deciliter	decigram
0.01 x basic unit	centimeter	centiliter	centigram
0.001 x basic unit	millimeter	milliliter	milligram

EXERCISES

Use the relationships given on page 64 to answer the following questions:

1. a. How many grams are equivalent to $\frac{1}{2}$ lb? $8 \times 28.35 = 226.8$
    b. How many liters are equivalent to 1 gallon? $4 \times 0.9464 = 3.7856$
    c. How many meters are equivalent to 1 yard? $36 \times 0.0254 = 0.9144$

2. Given that the bushel is 32 dry quarts, how many liters are equivalent to 1 bushel? $32 \times 1.101 = 35.232$

3. 10 hot dogs weigh 1 pound.
    Find, in grams, the weight of 1 hot dog. $453.6 \div 10 = 45.36$

4. Given that 1 mile is 1,760 yards:
    a. How many meters are equivalent to 1 mile? $1760 \times 0.9144 = 1609.344$
    b. How many kilometers are equivalent to 1 mile? $1609 \div 1,000 = 1.609$

D

Level 13

23   METRIC UNITS OF LENGTH

In the metric system, the basic unit of length is the meter. The French scientists calculated the distance from the north pole to the equator along the curved surface of the Earth. They took 1-millionth of this distance as the meter. A platinum bar whose length is 1 meter was made and kept as a model for the standard basic unit of length.

- Using the decimal system of numeration, larger and smaller units of length were developed.

a. For larger units:

     A unit 10 meters long was called decameter.

     A unit 100 meters long was called a hectometer.

     A unit 1000 meters long was called a kilometer.

b. For smaller units:

     A unit 1-tenth of a meter long was called a decimeter.

     A unit 1-hundredth of a meter long was called a centimeter.

     A unit 1-thousandth of a meter long was called a millimeter.

- The following chart shows how the other standard measures of length are related to the meter.

Kilometers (1000 meters)	Hectometer (100 meters)	Decameter (10 meters)	METER	Decimeter (0.1 meter)	Centimeter (0.01 meter)	Millimeter (0.001 meter)

- You may use the following chart.

Kilo	Hecto	Deca	METER	Deci	Centi	Milli

with the understanding that:

     Kilo refers to kilometer which is 1000 meters,

     Hecto refers to hectometer which is 100 meters,

     Deca refers to decameter which is 10 meters,

     Deci refers to decimeter which is 1-tenth of the meter,

     Centi refers to centimeter which is 1-hundredth of the meter,

     Milli refers to millimeter which is 1-thousandth of the meter.

- This chart is similar to the place value chart.

1000's	100's	10's	ONES	10ths	100ths	1000ths

- The relationships of any unit to the one to the right and to the left still hold:

     1 kilometer = 10 hectometers   1 meter = 10 decimeters

     1 hectometer = 10 decameters   1 decimeter = 10 centimeters

     1 decameter = 10 meters   1 centimeter = 10 millimeters

- You can use these relationships to find out how a unit is related to any other unit.

Using the following chart:

Kilo	Hecto	Deca	METER	Deci	Centi	Milli

You can find out how one unit is related to another.

Examples:

1 decameter	= 10 meters		1 kilometer	= 10 hectometers
	= 100 decimeters			= 100 decameters
	= 1,000 centimeters			= 1,000 meters
	= 10,000 millimeters			= 10,000 decimeters
1 decimeter	= 10 centimeters		1 hectometer	= 10 decameters
	= 100 millimeters			= 100 meters

APPLICATIONS

Fill in the units in the chart below, and then use it to answer the questions.

Kilometer (1000 meters)	Hectometer (100 meters)	Decameter (10 meters)	METER	Decimeter (0.1 meter)	Centimeter (0.01 meter)	Millimeter (0.001 meter)

1. a. How many centimeters are in 1 hectometer?   <u>10,000</u>
   b. How many decimeters are in 1 hectometer?   <u>1,000</u>
   c. How many decimeters are in 1 decameter?   <u>100</u>
   d. How many decameters are in 1 kilometer?   <u>100</u>
   e. How many centimeters are in 1 kilometer?   <u>100,000</u>
   f. How many millimeters are in 1 kilometer?   <u>1,000,000</u>
   g. How many centimeters are in 1 decameter?   <u>1,000</u>
   h. How many millimeters are in 1 hectometer?   <u>100,000</u>

2. a. What fraction of the meter is the centimeter?   <u>0.01</u>
   b. What fraction of the kilometer is the meter?   <u>0.001</u>
   c. What fraction of the decameter is the decimeter?   <u>0.01</u>
   d. What fraction of the kilometer is the decameter?   <u>0.01</u>
   e. What fraction of the meter is the millimeter?   <u>0.001</u>
   f. What fraction of the decameter is the centimeter?   <u>0.001</u>
   g. What fraction of the hectometer is the centimeter?   <u>0.0001</u>
   h. What fraction of the kilometer is the decimeter?   <u>0.0001</u>

D

Knowing how a unit is related to a smaller unit, you can convert any measure in a unit to a measure in the smaller unit.

Example 1.

How many centimeters are in 5.4 meters?

Discussion:

- You first find out how the meter and the centimeter are related.

    1 meter = 100 centimeters

- Knowing that 1 meter is 100 centimeters, change 5.4 meters into centimeters:

    5.4 meters = 5.4 x 100 = 540 centimeters

Example 2.

How many decimeters are in 3.8 hectometers?

Solution:

- Using the chart: 1 hectometer = 1000 decimeters.
- 3.8 hectometers = 3.8 x 1000 = 3800 decimeters.

You also can convert a measure in a unit into a measure in a larger unit.

Example 3.

How many meters are in 28 millimeters?

Discussion:

- You first find out how the meter and the millimeter are related.

    1 meter = 1,000 millimeters

- Knowing that 1,000 millimeters make 1 meter, change 28 millimeters into meters:

    28 millimeters = 28 ÷ 1,000 = 0.028 meters

You also can think another way:

- 1 millimeter is 1-thousandth of a meter.
- 28 millimeters are 28 thousandths of a meter.

    28 millimeters = 0.028 meter

Example 4.

How many decameters are in 345 decimeters?

Solution 1:

- Using the chart: 1 decameter = 100 decimeters.
- 345 decimeters = 345 ÷ 100 = 3.45 decameters.

Solution 2:

- Using the chart: 1 decimeter is 1-hundredth of the decameter.
- 345 decimeters = 345 hundredths of 1 decameter = 3.45 decameters

D

APPLICATIONS

Write the equation:

1. How many centimeters are in:
   a. 2.7 meters? $2.7 \times 100 = 270$
   b. 3.45 decameters? $3.45 \times 1000 = 3450$
   c. 294 millimeters? $294 \div 10 = 29.4$

2. How many decimeters are in:
   a. 5.48 hectometers? $5.48 \times 1000 = 5480$
   b. 8.94 decameters? $8.94 \times 100 = 894$
   c. 765 centimeters? $765 \div 10 = 76.5$

3. How many millimeters are in:
   a. 3.98 centimeters? $3.98 \times 10 = 39.8$
   b. 2.59 meters? $2.59 \times 1000 = 2590$
   c. 3.8 decameters? $3.8 \times 10,000 = 38000$

4. How many kilometers are in:
   a. 57 decameters? $57 \div 100 = 0.57$
   b. 386 meters? $386 \div 1,000 = 0.368$
   c. 698 hectometers? $698 \div 10 = 69.8$

5. How many meters are in:
   a. 29 centimeters? $29 \div 100 = 0.29$
   b. 3976 millimeters? $3976 \div 1,000 = 3.976$
   c. 4.89 hectometers? $4.89 \times 100 = 489$

6. AB and BC are two roads. AB is 1.82 kilometers long and BC is 989 meters long. How many hectometers is it from A to C through B?

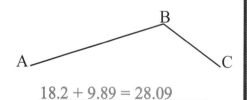

   $18.2 + 9.89 = 28.09$

7. A factory produced 100,000 pieces of wire. Each piece was 3.78 centimeters long. Given that 45 meters of wire were wasted, how many kilometers of wire were used?

   a. $100,000 \times 3.78 = 378000$ cm
   b. 378000 cm $= 3.78$ km
   c. $3.78 + 0.045 = 3.825$ km

D

Level 13

THE METRIC RULER

Most rulers, especially the ones you use in school, have one edge marked in inches and each inch is divided into sixteenths.

The other edge is divided into centimeters and each centimeter is divided into tenths. Each tenths of 1 centimeter is a millimeter. This edge is marked into centimeters and millimeters as shown.

- A stick 1 meter long is 100 times as long as the distance AB on the ruler.

You can use the ruler to measure any given length or to locate two points a given distance apart.

Example 1.

 Measure the length AB.

Discussion:

 To make an accurate measurement you have to be careful.

- Place your ruler so that its edge coincides with line AB.
- Adjust the ruler so that point A coincides with the "0" mark.
- Find the point on the edge of the ruler which coincides with point B. Find the mark which is the closest to B.
 B is between the two marks "5" and "6".

 Line segment AB is 5 centimeters and 1 millimeter long.

Example 2.

 Draw a line segment XY which is 3.6 centimeters long.

Discussion: X

- 3.6 centimeters is the same as 3 centimeters and 6 millimeters.
- Adjust your ruler so that X coincides with the "0" mark.
- Start at point X and draw a line that stops at the mark 3 centimeters and 6 millimeters.

1. Use your ruler to find the length in centimeters and millimeters:

    a. AB is __7__ cm and __9__ mm.

    b. BC is __6__ cm and __5__ mm.

    c. CD is __4__ cm and __0__ mm.

    d. AD is __7__ cm and __5__ mm.

    e. AC is __5__ cm and __0__ mm.

    f. BD is __3__ cm and __2__ mm.

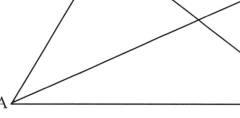

2. Draw line segments of the given length:

    a. Draw a line segment XY whose length is 7cm and 8 millimeters.

    X

    b. Draw a line segment MN whose length is 8 centimeters and 2 millimeters.

    M

    c. Draw a line segment AZ whose lenght is 14 centimeters and 2 millimeters.

    A

3. Use you ruler:

    a. In centimeters what length is
       equivalent to 4 inches?   __10.1 cm__

    b. In inches, what length is equivalent to 16
       centimeters and 5 millimeters? $6\frac{1}{2}$ inches

    c. How long is the line segment AB in centimeters?   __3.8__

    A———————————————— B

4. Study the figure to the right.

    a. If you make AB and AC coincide (with B
       between A and C), how long will BC be?

    b. If you make AB and AC a straight line (with
       A between B and C), how long will BC be?

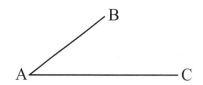

       AB = 2.8cm   AC = 4.5cm   a. 1.7cm   b. 7.3cm

71

Level 13

24 METRIC UNITS OF CAPACITY

- In the metric system, the basic unit of capacity is the "liter".
  The liter is the capacity of a cube whose edges
  are 1 decimeter (10 centimeters) long.

- The other units of capacity are:

  a. 1 Decaliter = 10 liters   b. 1 Deciliter = 0.1 liter
     1 Hectoliter = 100 liters   1 Centiliter = 0.01 liter
     1 Kiloliter = 1000 liters   1 Milliliter = 0.001 liter

- The following chart is similar to the one we have used for the metric units of length.

KILOLITER (1000 liters)	HECTOLITER (100 liters)	DECALITER (10 liters)	LITER	DECILITER (0.1 liter)	CENTILITER (0.01 liter)	MILLILITER (0.001 liter)

- You also may use the shortened chart shown below:

Kilo	Hecto	Deca	LITER	Deci	Centi	Milli

- You can find out how a unit is related to any other unit.

Examples:

1. a. 1 Liter = 10 deciliters
   = <u>100</u> centiliters
   = <u>1000</u> millilters

   b. 1 Decaliter = 10 liters
   = <u>100</u> deciliters
   = <u>1000</u> centiliters
   = <u>10,000</u> milliliters

   c. 1 Deciliter = 10 centiliters
   = <u>100</u> millimeters

   d. 1 Kiloliter = 10 hectoliters
   = <u>100</u> decaliters
   = <u>1000</u> liters

2. a. 1 milliliter = 0.1 centiliter
   = <u>0.01</u> deciliter
   = <u>0.001</u> liter

   b. 1 deciliter = <u>0.1</u> liter
   = <u>0.01</u> decaliter
   = <u>0.001</u> hectoliter
   = <u>0.0001</u> kiloliter

   c. 1 decaliter = <u>0.1</u> hectoliter
   = <u>0.01</u> kiloliter

   d. 1 liter = <u>0.1</u> decaliter
   = <u>0.01</u> hectoliter
   = <u>0.001</u> kiloliter

D

APPLICATIONS

1. To the right is the picture of a container composed of two cubes whose edges are 10 centimeters long. What is the capacity of the container in liters?

   <u>2 liters</u>

2. To the right is the picture of a container whose edges are 30, 20, and 10 centimeters long. Find the capacity in liters.

   <u>3 x 2 x 1 = 6</u>

3. To the right is the picture of a container whose edges are 40, 30, and 20 centimeters long. Find the capacity in liters.

   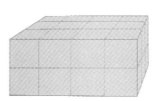

   <u>4 x 3 x 2 = 24</u>

4. a. How many centiliters are in 1 hectoliter? <u>10,000</u>
   b. How many deciliters are in 1 hectoliter? <u>1,000</u>
   c. How many deciliters are in 1 decaliter? <u>100</u>
   d. How many decaliters are in 1 kiloliter? <u>100</u>
   e. How many centiliters are in 1 kiloliter? <u>100,000</u>
   f. How many milliliters are in 1 kiloliter? <u>1,000,000</u>
   g. How many centiliters are in 1 decaliter? <u>1,000</u>
   h. How many milliliters are in 1 hectoliter? <u>100,000</u>

5. a. What fraction of the liter is the centiliter? <u>0.01</u>
   b. What fraction of the kiloliter is the liter? <u>0.001</u>
   c. What fraction of the decaliter is the deciliter? <u>0.01</u>
   d. What fraction of the kiloliter is the decaliter? <u>0.01</u>
   e. What fraction of the liter is the milliliter? <u>0.001</u>
   f. What fraction of the decaliter is the centiliter? <u>0.001</u>
   g. What fraction of the hectoliter is the centiliter? <u>0.0001</u>
   h. What fraction of the decaliter is the milliliter? <u>0.0001</u>

D

Level 13

Knowing how a unit of capacity is related to another, you can convert a measure in one unit into a measure in the other unit.

KILOLITER (1000 liters)	HECTOLITER (100 liters)	DECALITER (10 liters)	LITER	DECILITER (0.1 liter)	CENTILITER (0.01 liter)	MILLILITER (0.001 meter)

Example 1.

How many liters are in 4.89 decaliters?

Solution:

- Using the chart: 1 decaliter = 10 liters
- 4.89 decaliters = 4.89 x 10 = 48.9 liters

Example 2.

How many milliliters are in 3.72 liters?

Solution:

- Using the chart: 1 liter = 1000 milliliters
- 3.72 liters = 3.72 x 1,000 = 3720 milliliters

Example 3.

How many hectoliters are in 798 deciliters?

Solution:

- Using the chart: 1 hectoliter = 1,000 deciliters
- 798 deciliters = 798 ÷ 1,000 = 0.798 hectoliters

APPLICATIONS

Write the equation:

1. How many liters are in:
   a. 5.7 kiloliters? — $5.7 \times 1000 = 5700$
   b. 38 hectoliters? — $38 \times 100 = 3800$
   c. 7.04 decaliters? — $7.04 \times 10 = 70.4$

2. How many centiliters are in:
   a. 46 liters? — $46 \times 100 = 4600$
   b. 3.86 decaliters? — $3.86 \times 1,000 = 3860$
   c. 297 milliliters? — $297 \div 10 = 29.7$

3. How many decaliters are in:
   a. 65.3 liters? — $65.3 \div 10 = 6.53$
   b. 8.58 kiloliters? — $8.58 \times 100 = 858$
   c. 0.27 deciliters? — $0.27 \div 100 = 0.0027$

D

4. A car runs 6.24 kilometers on 1 liter of gas.
   How far can it go on 1 hectoliter of gas?

   _100 x 6.24 = 624 km_

5. 1 liter of fuel weighs 0.95 kilogram.
   Find the weight of 1 kiloliter of fuel.

   _1000 x 0.95 = 950 kg_

6. 1 liter of milk weighs 0.92 kg.
   Find the weight of 1 deciliter of milk.

   _0.92 ÷ 10 = 0.092 kg_

7. A chemist prepared a prescription which measured
   2.25 liters. He used the drug to fill bottles whose
   capacity is 25 centiliters.

   a. 2.25 liters = 225 centiliters

   How many bottles did he use?

   b. 225 ÷ 25 = 9 bottles

8. A, B, and C are three containers.
   The capacity of A is 4.5 liters, of B 360 centiliters,
   and of C 0.9 decaliters. If you fill A and B and
   then pour the contents into C, what is the capacity

   a. 4.5 + 3.6 = 8.1 liters

   of the empty part of C?

   b. 9 - 8.1 = 0.9 liters

9. The contents of a jar fill a 100-milliliter
   flask 75 times.

   75 x 100 = 7500 milliliters

   Find the capacity of the jar in liters.

   7500 milliliters = 7.5 liters

10. The inside dimensions of a box are
    40 cm, 30cm, and 10 cm.
    Find, in liters, the capacity of the box.

    _4 x 3 x 1= 12_

11. The dimensions of an aquarium are 50 cm,
    40 cm, and 30 cm.

    a. 5 x 4 x 3 = 60 liters

    Find the capacity of the aquarium in kiloliters.

    b. 60 liters = 0.060 kiloliter

12. The inside dimensions of a box are
    1 meter, 70 centimeters, and 4 decimeters.

    a. 10 x 7 x 4 = 280 liters

    Find, in deciliters, the capacity of the box.

    b. 280 liters = 2800 deciliters

D

Level 13

25 METRIC UNITS OF WEIGHT

In the metric system, the basic unit is the gram. Related to the gram, the other units are:

- 1 decagram = 10 grams
- 1 hectogram = 100 grams
- 1 kilogram = 1,000 grams

- 1 decigram = 0.1 gram
- 1 centigram = 0.01 gram
- 1 milligram = 0.001 gram

The following chart represents the relationship listed above.

KILOGRAM (1000 gram)	HECTOGRAM (100 gram)	DECAGRAM (10 gram)	GRAM	DECIGRAM (0.1 gram)	CENTIGRAM (0.01gram)	MILLIGRAM (0.001 gram)

You may also use the shortened chart:

Kilo	Hecto	Deca	GRAM	Deci	Centi	Milli

Using the chart, you can find out how any unit is related to any other unit.

Examples:

a. 1 decagram = 10 grams
           = <u>100</u> decigrams
           = <u>1,000</u> centigrams

b. 1 decigram = 10 centigrams
           = <u>100</u> milligrams

c. 1 kilogram = 10 hectograms
           = <u>100</u> decagrams
           = <u>1,000</u> grams
           = <u>10,000</u> decigrams
           = <u>100,000</u> centigrams
           = <u>1,000,000</u> milligrams

The Metric Ton

This unit is a large unit, equivalent to 1,000 kilograms, which is used in measuring the weight of very heavy objects, such as the weight of a ship, and the product of a farm or a factory.

You can find out how the metric ton is related to other units of weight:

       1 ton = 1,000 kilograms
            = <u>10,000</u> hectograms
            = <u>100,000</u> decagrams
            = <u>1,000,000</u> grams

Example.

Find, in metric tons, the total weight of 100 boxes, 25.8 kg each.

Solution:

100 boxes weigh 100 x 25.8 = 2,580 kg

2,580 kg = 2,580 ÷ 1000 = 2.580 tons

D

APPLICATIONS

1. How many grams are in:
   a. 5.37 hectograms?
   b. 2.41 kilograms?
   c. 8594 centigrams?
   d. 36.4 milligrams?

   a. 5.37 x 100 = 537
   b. 2.41 x 1,000 = 2410
   c. 8594 ÷ 100 = 85.94
   d. 36.4 ÷ 1,000 = 0.0364

2. A sheet of paper weighs 2.1 grams. Find the weight of 500 sheets of this paper in kilograms.

   a. 500 x 2.1 = 1050 grams
   b. 1050 grams = 1.05 kilograms

3. A chemist had 600 bottles; the weight of each was 9.2 grams. Find the total weight in kilograms.

   wrong a. 600 x 9.2 = 5880 grams 5520
   b. 5880 grams = 5.880 kilograms
   5.52 kg

4. A wholesale butcher had 5.2 tons of meat. He sold 2800 kilograms of the meat he had. How much meat did he have left?

   a. 5.2 tons = 5200 kilograms
   b. 5200 - 2800 = 2400 kilograms

5. 200 identical boxes weigh 3.8 metric tons. Find the weight of 12 boxes.

   a. 3.8 tons = 3800 kg
   b. 3800 ÷ 200 = 19 kg
   c. 12 x 19 = 208 kg

6. Find, in kilograms, the sum of 28 decagrams and 7000 grams.

   a. 28 decagrams = 0.28 kg
   b. 7000 grams = 7 kg
   c. 0.28 + 7 = 7.28 kg

7. Find, in kilograms, the difference between 380 hectograms and 2 metric tons.

   a. 380 hectograms = 38 kg
   b. 2 tons = 2000 kg
   c. 2000 - 38 = 1962 kg

8. A farmer has two lots of corn: 3.1 metric tons, and 7,590 kilograms. How much corn does he have?

   a. 7,590 kg = 7.59 tons
   b. 3.10 + 7.59 = 10.69 tons

9. 1,000 boxes, 2.68 kg each were loaded on a truck which weighed 8.96 metric tons. Find the total weight.

   a. 1,000 x 2.68 = 2680 kg = 2.68 tons
   b. 8.96 + 2.68 = 11.64 tons

D

Level 13

UNIT D TEST

1. In the metric system, what is the basic unit used to measure:
   a. Length? __meter__   b. Capacity? __liter__   c. Weight? __gram__

2. In the metric system, six prefixes are used. What are they, and what do they indicate?

Deca = 10 x basic unit	Deci = 0.1 basic unit
Hecto = 100 x basic unit	Centi = 0.01 basic unit
Kilo = 1,000 x basic unit	Milli = 0.001 basic unit

3. The Metric System of Measures is based on the place value system. Show how.

   Each unit is 10 times the smaller unit, and 1-tenth the next larger unit.

4. Given: 1 liquid quart = 0.9464 liter:
   How many liters are equal to 1 pint? $0.9464 \div 2 = 0.4732$

5. The distance between two villages is 10 miles.
   Given: 1 yard = 0.9144 meter, what is the distance in kilometers?
   a. 1 mile = 1760 x 0.9144 = 1.609 Km
   b. 10 miles = 10 x 1.609 = 16.09 Km

6. A parcel weighs 2 pounds and 8 ounces.
   Given: 1 ounce = 28.35 grams, find the weight of the parcel in kilograms.
   a. (2 x 16) + 8 = 40 ounces
   b. 40 x 28.35 = 1134 gm = 1.134 kg

7. Fill in the chart below to represent the metric units of length.

Kilometer (1000 meters)	Hectometer (100 meters)	Decameter (10 meters)	METER	Decimeter (0.1 meter)	Centimeter (0.01 meter)	Millimeter (0.001 meter)

   a. How many centimeters are in 1 hectometer?   __10,000__
   b. How many decimeters are in 1 kilometer?   __10,000__
   c. How many millimeters are in 1 decameter?   __10,000__

8. How many decimeters are in 5.83 kilometers? $5.83 \times 10,000 = 58,300$
   How many kilometers are in 3974 meters? $3974 \div 1,000 = 3.974$

9. In a factory, a wire 2.43 km long was cut into pieces, each 75 cm long. Did any wire remain?
   a. 2.43km = 243,000cm
   b. 243,000 ÷ 75 = 3,240 pieces
   No wire remained

10. Fill in the chart below to represent the metric units of capacity:

Kiloliter (1000 liters)	Hectoliter (100 liters)	Decaliter (10 liters)	LITER	Deciliter (0.1 literr)	Centiliter (0.01 liter)	Milliliter (0.001 liter)

    a. How many centiliters are in 1 kiloliter? <u>100,000</u>

    b. How many deciliters are in 1 hectoliter? <u>1,000</u>

    c. How many centiliters are in 1 hectoliter? <u>10,000</u>

11. How many deciliters are in 2.34 kiloliters? <u>$2.34 \times 10,000 = 23,400$</u>

    How many hectoliters are in 784 centiliters? <u>$784 \div 10,000 = 0.0784$</u>

12. In a perfume factory, 1.26 kiloliters of a certain formula were produced. How many 100-centiliter bottles would be filled?

    a. <u>1.26 kiloliters = 126,000 centiliters</u>

    b. <u>$126,000 \div 100 = 1,260$ bottles</u>

13. Fill in the chart below to represent the metric units of weight.

Kilogram (1000 grams)	Hectogram (100 grams)	Decagram (10 grams)	GRAM	Decigram (0.1 gram)	Centigram (0.01 gram)	Milligram (0.001 gram)

    a. How many centigrams are in 1 hectogram? <u>10,000</u>

    b. How many decigrams are in 1 decagram? <u>100</u>

    c. How many milligrams are in 1 kilogram? <u>1,000,000</u>

14. How many centigrams are in 8.56 kilograms? <u>$8.56 \times 100,000 = 856,000$</u>

    How many kilograms are in 375 decigrams? <u>$375 \div 10,000 = 0.0375$</u>

15. 100 cream jars, 175 gm each, were packed in a box that weighed 3.25 kg. Find the weight of the shipment.

    a. $100 \times 0.175 = 17.5$ kg

    b. $17.5 + 3.25 = 20.75$ kg

16. a. How many kilograms are in 1 metric ton? <u>1,000 kg</u>

    b. How many kilograms are in 2.64 tons? <u>$2.64 \times 1,000 = 2640$ kg</u>

    c. How many tons are in 7692 kilograms? <u>$7692 \div 1,000 = 7.692$ tons</u>

17. 100 boxes, 13.47 kg each, are loaded on a truck which weighs 4.75 tons. Find the total weight of the truck loaded.

    a. <u>$100 \times 13.47 = 1347$ kg $= 1.347$ tons</u>

    b. <u>$4.75 + 1.347 = 6.097$ tons</u>

D

18. 1 mile is approximately 1.61 kilometers.
    a. How many kilometers are in 100 miles?   <u>161 kilometers</u>
       (1.61 x 100) kilometers

    b. How many miles are in 56.35 kilometers?   <u>35 miles</u>
       (56.35 ÷ 1.61) miles

19. 1 inch is 2.54 centimeters?
    a. How many centimeters are in 1 foot?   <u>30.49 centimeters</u>
       (2.54 x 12) centimeters

    b. How many inches are in 1 meter.   <u>39.35 inches</u>
       (100 ÷ 2.54) inches

20. 1 kilogram is 2.25 pounds.
    a. How many pounds are in 72.5 kilograms?   <u>163.125 pounds</u>
       (2.25 x 72.5) pounds

    b. How many kilograms are in 67.5 pounds?   <u>30 kilograms</u>
       (67.5 ÷ 2.54) kilograms

21. A 2 liter bottle of Coke contains 67.6 fluid ounces.
    a. How many fluid ounces are in 1 case of 6 bottles of Coke?   <u>405.6 fluid ounces</u>
       (67.5 x 6) fluid ounces

    b. How many centiliters are in 1 fluid ounce?   <u>2.96 centiliters</u>
       (200 ÷ 67.6) centiliters